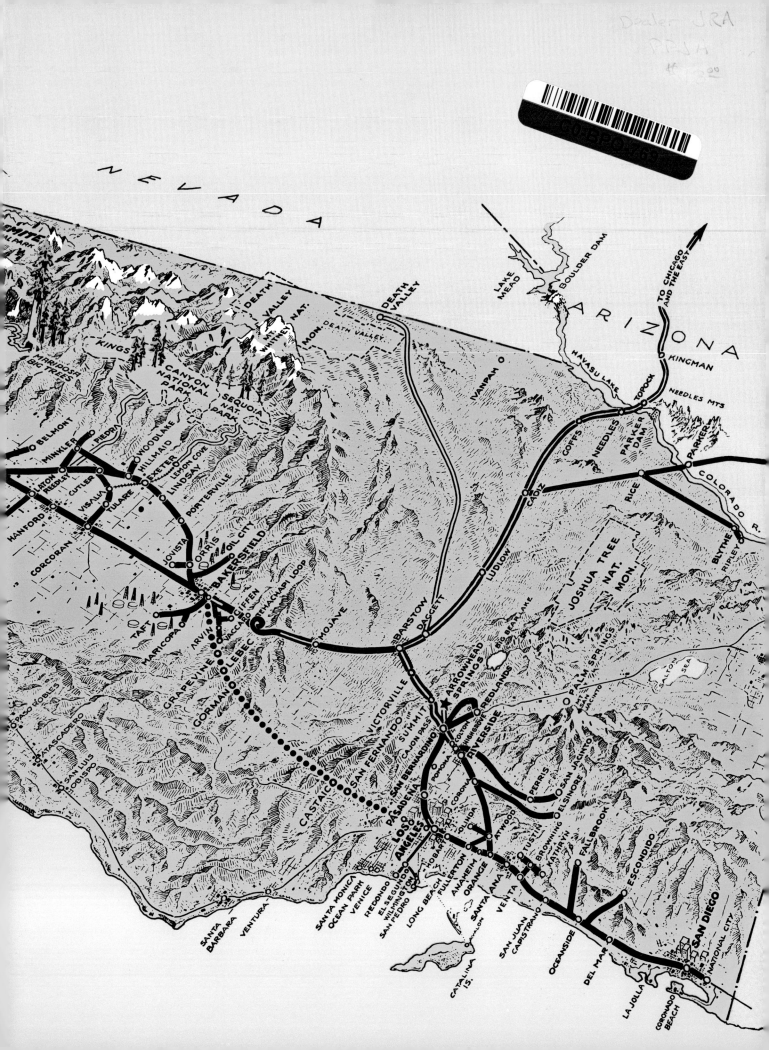

Santa Fe

...Steel Rails Through California

Donald Duke and Stan Kistler

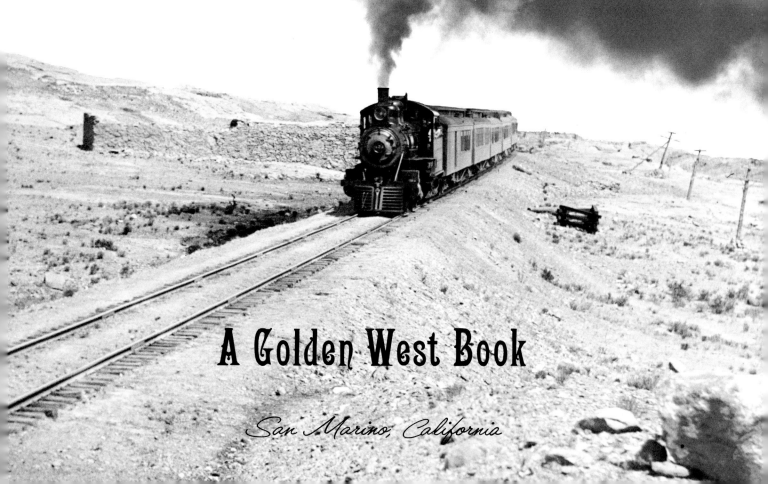

A Golden West Book

San Marino, California

A C K N O W L E D G M E N T S

For picture material contributed to this book, either of their own photographic artistry or from collections of which they are owners or custodians, the authors are in debt of the following: Jim Ady, Gerald M. Best, W. C. Hendrick, Phillips C. Kauke, Fred Matthews, R. P. Middlebrook, Joe Moir, Al Rose, R. E. Searle, Chard Walker, W. C. Whittaker, Mrs. Shirley Davis of the Title Insurance & Trust Co.— Union Title Office, Clyde Simpson of the Security First National Bank of Los Angeles, and the State Historical Society of Colorado, and to all others whose names appear in the credits. In extra measure to John B. Hungerford and David Myrick for historical background and technical assistance. The authors owe special personal gratitude to H. P. "Hank" O'Leary of the public relations staff of the Santa Fe for assistance and enthusiasm. Also to Frank E. Meitz and staff of the Santa Fe film and photographic bureau for their photographic fruits. Finally to Harlan Hiney and Stan Repp, better perhaps than any artists, seem to the authors of this book to comprehend the glory of Santa Fe steam and thrill of streamliners.

Golden West Books

A Division of Pacific Railroad Publications, Inc.

P.O. BOX 8136 • SAN MARINO, CALIFORNIA • 91108

JIM ADY

California . . . a land of limitless miles and high altitudes and there were locomotives to match.

INTRODUCTION TO Santa Fe ...Steel Rail

The name Santa Fe began with the early history of the Southwest, grew with the flow of commerce that followed the Santa Fe Trail, and has been popularized into a household term by the Santa Fe Railway. Today, more than ever, it is associated with the thought of places to go and the famous fleet of streamlined trains.

Without the Santa Fe Railway, the social and economic development of the great American West might have been retarded. Nature, indeed, had endowed the area with fabulous riches and boundless opportunities, but in doing so, scattered the gifts over an enormous landlocked territory. There they could have remained, isolated and unused indefinitely, had it not been for the coming of the rails.

Even after the steam locomotive had proved itself technically feasible, the building of the Santa Fe was more than a matter of laying track and furnishing equipment whenever or wherever traffic might warrant it. There were problems in every new region. Labor was scarce and unskilled. It was difficult to obtain supplies and to overcome mountain barriers. Communication was slow and uncertain and many misunderstandings developed. Competition among railroads became violent and unrestrained, with constant threat during and after construction.

Yet somehow the Santa Fe network was built, and at a speed without parallel in recorded history. The treasures of the West were opened and people from all over the world began to come. A whole new society, distinctive in outlook and talent, came into being.

Many books have been devoted to the history of a particular railroad or railroads in general, but except for technical works and limited historical societies' publications little has been compiled showing the history of a railroad within a given state. In a way this is not strange, since the scant information of historical nature available has been limited to material in the hands of a few collectors and specialists. Therefore, such information is seldom encountered by the average person.

This volume began life as a general pictorial history of the Santa Fe Railway System. In gathering and compiling this record, the authors found so much historical information, anecdotes and pictorial quality about their home State of California that it was decided to divide the history of the Santa Fe into sections and make each volume complete.

In the days gone by the Santa Fe found a home in the State of California. It named its finest flyer for it, the *California Limited*. It conquered Cajon Pass and the mighty Tehachapi. Its rails stretched along the shores of the Pacific between the Pueblo of Los Angeles and Mission San Diego de Alcala. Wherever commerce took it one found the Santa Fe.

California has always been a land of great contrasts. It has the highest mountains, the hottest deserts, the tallest and oldest trees. It has great cities, natural harbors, vast forests, orange groves and vineyards. It has Hollywood and the Golden Gate. It has the yellow gold of the Mother Lode, the green gold of the San Joaquin Valley ranches and the black gold called oil.

Since the first train crossed the California border with its red plush and polished brass, the Santa Fe has been a part of California. With its coming it brought some of the world's largest locomotives and the finest transcontinental trains. Today its great streamlined trains continue to make California and the West their home.

What better location, what finer railroad institution could find permanency between these hard covers?

DONALD DUKE
STAN KISTLER

JUNE, 1963

"California . . . lies beyond those mountains and we shall never be able to reach it," wrote John Bidwell, leader of

the first overland emigrant train in his journal on October 29, 1841. As late as 1862, California was for all intents and purposes still isolated from the rest of the United States. Travel to California was possible only by ship by way of Cape Horn, by jungle route across Panama or seventeen days of punishment on the Overland Stage, barring washouts, Indian attacks and other perils.

Little more than a hundred years ago President Lincoln signed the Pacific Railroad Bill on July 1, 1862, thus providing for construction of a railroad from the Missouri River to the Pacific Coast. Completion of the first transcontinental railroad with the driving of the last spike joining the tracks of the Central Pacific and Union Pacific railroads at Promontory, Utah, opened up the West for the first time.

The Central Pacific properties were taken over by the Southern Pacific by 1885. During the next several years Southern Pacific rails covered most of California like a web. Lines of railroad spread rapidly north to Portland, Oregon, and southwest into Texas with an eye on the entire South. The Southern Pacific had emerged into a huge railroad network. It controlled not only all the railroads of California, but great steamship lines as well. The command of the Southern Pacific became law on the Pacific Coast.

Freight rates on the lines of the Southern Pacific were high, but without them merchandise could not be moved to market. The aspirations of any small railroad builder seeking a tidewater terminal in California were either met at the California border with a closed door, or some means was undertaken to buy the lines out or see that the railroad was financially destroyed. Southern Pacific had the State of California to itself. It controlled foreign trade, rail, sea transportation, and the political life.

A small group of men met in conclave during the early days of 1858, in the frontier town of Atchison, Kansas. The subject of discussion was a new railroad to attract settlers to the great plains of the middle American West fringing the winding Santa Fe Trail. On February 11, 1859, the necessary charter to build the Atchison & Topeka Railroad was granted by the legislature of the State of Kansas. According to the title, the northern end of the steel highway was to rest on the west bank of the Missouri River, opposite St. Joseph, while the other terminus was to be at Topeka, 50 miles to the southwest.

Eighteen months passed before the next step was taken, and then the preliminary capital was obtained only after each of the thirteen men at the meeting subscribed and became directors of the company. Nothing transpired for four years beyond the change of the title to the Atchison, Topeka & Santa Fe Railroad. The Federal Government then passed an

Act granting three million acres of land along the proposed route. The one proviso was completion of the rail line to the Colorado border by December 31, 1872, if the Santa Fe wished to take advantage of this land grant.

Colonel Cyrus K. Holliday, father of the scheme, visualized a line with its extremities resting on Chicago, the Atlantic seaboard and San Francisco Bay. Many exclaimed, "The darned old fool!" The rails continued to move west. By December 1869, the rails had been laid some 21 miles and the equipment consisted of a second hand locomotive, a coach and twelve flat cars. The end of the year was drawing close and so was the Colorado border. The land grant secured, all apprehensions concerning the future of the road vanished. Leisurely the Santa Fe considered extensions toward the Rocky Mountains and Santa Fe on the west, and to Kansas City on the east. "On to Santa Fe" was echoed up and down the grade. But as the capital was approached the engineers found extremely broken country, through which it was found physically impossible to carry a railroad to the frontier town. Santa Fe could not be planted on the main line to vindicate the title, so the engineers doubled back to Lamy and from that point a branch eighteen miles in length was built.

Continuing their western progress, the Santa Fe at last reached Albuquerque, New Mexico. Here a pause was made to re-examine the preliminary surveys. To conquer the desert ahead was no easy task. There were few towns along the old Santa Fe Trail. Boiling heat, blowing sand and unfriendly bands of Indians were the welcome mat for the new railroad. The mighty Southern Pacific was ready for any renegade railroad builder who wished to crack the wall around its supremacy over California. The pathfinders of the Santa Fe decided to sit it out.

The way to the Pacific began to open again with the acquisition of the franchise of the Atlantic & Pacific Railroad. The Atlantic & Pacific Company was created by Act of Congress July 1866, and its capital stock fixed at one hundred million dollars. The act authorized a line of railway from Springfield, Missouri, to the western boundary of Missouri; then by the most eligible route to a point on the Canadian River in Indian Territory; then to Albuquerque on the Rio Grande; then by a suitable pass to the headwaters of the Colorado; then along

JAY GOULD OF THE TEXAS & PACIFIC

COLLIS P. HUNTINGTON OF THE SOUTHERN PACIFIC

U.S. SUPREME COURT

Huntington and Gould had secretly purchased a controlling interest in the St. Louis & San Francisco Railway and were in a strategic position to prevent further expansion of the Atlantic & Pacific.

the 35th parallel of latitude to the Colorado River at such points suitable for crossing; then by the most practicable route to the Pacific Ocean. By this act there was granted a right of way through public lands to the extent of 100 feet on each side of the railroad, together with grounds for stations, shops, depots. Such grounds were exempted from taxation within the Territories of the United States.

Prior to September 1876, the Atlantic & Pacific Company had built or acquired 293 miles of road, extending from Pacific to Seneca in the State of Missouri. By reasons of default in the payment of interest the property in Missouri was sold under foreclosure to William F. Buckley, and in November of that year all rights were conveyed to the St. Louis & San Francisco Railway Company.

In 1879, negotiations were begun between the Santa Fe and the St. Louis & San Francisco regarding the rehabilitation of the Atlantic & Pacific Company and the completion under its charter to the Pacific Coast. By an accord known as the *Tripartite Agreement,* dated January 31, 1880, one-half of the capital stock of the Atlantic & Pacific Company then

owned by the St. Louis & San Francisco Railway Company was transferred to the Atchison, Topeka & Santa Fe Railroad. Construction of the Western Division was promptly launched under the banner of the Atlantic & Pacific Railroad. The railhead was pushed across New Mexico, crossing the continental divide east of Gallup.

Late in 1881, the Santa Fe made its second subscription payment of fifteen million on the Atlantic & Pacific bonds. It was astonished to discover that Jay Gould and C. P. Huntington had secretly purchased a controlling interest in the St. Louis & San Francisco Railway and were in a strategic position to prevent further rapid expansion of the Atlantic & Pacific Railroad. Huntington wished to preserve his California empire by delaying the building of the Atlantic & Pacific beyond the Needles on the California border. Gould's connection with the enterprise was purely a financial investment. The Southern Pacific vigorously and quickly began the construction of a line from Mojave southeast toward the Colorado River. The Santa Fe was obliged for the time being to accept the situation and continued

Atlantic & Pacific train No. 3 pauses for a photograph on the outskirts of the Needles, circa 1886. Locomotive No. 35, a hefty 4-4-0, built by Manchester in 1882 was named the *General McKenzie*. The 12-stall roundhouse, small machine shop and sandhouse illustrate this 1890 scene. The post office and station of the Atlantic & Pacific were established on February 18, 1883, on the Arizona side of the Colorado River and named after the near-by pinnacles. On October 11 of the same year, the railroad transferred the name to a new town on the California side, a location it considered better suited for a division point.

SANTA FE RAILWAY

to push its rails through Flagstaff, Williams, Ash Fork and Kingman in Arizona Territory.

From Kingman, the Santa Fe rails dipped down into the valley of the mighty Colorado and construction of a bridge was begun some twenty miles south of the Needles. On the western bank the Southern Pacific forces in their haste to reach the Colorado River ahead of the Atlantic & Pacific made a slight error in calculation. English iron rails had been laid east of Mojave for some miles, but the Atlantic & Pacific charter specified that American made steel rails must be used. Tracks were ripped up and relaid, yet the Southern Pacific still reached the Needles ahead of schedule.

On January 11, 1883, D. W. Kinsley of the government commission was questioned by the Boston Herald. He said, "The Atlantic & Pacific is a well-constructed railroad, excellent in location, running through interesting country. The road is well built, laid with 56-pound steel rails 30 feet long, averaging sixteen ties to the rail, fastened with double angle joints. Bridges are of wood and iron, first class in every respect, many marvels of engineering skill. The passenger equipment is of the latest patterns and improvements and the locomotives are of the most improved makes."

By July 12, 1883, the tracks of the Atlantic & Pacific were finished to a connection with the Southern Pacific at the Needles. Completion of the great through route to the Pacific would be opened upon completion of the bridge across the Colorado River. As the bridge neared completion, disagreements developed between Southern Pacific and Atlantic & Pacific officials. The Southern Pacific already had a route to the Pacific by way of Deming, New Mexico. However, this was considerably longer than over the new line by way of the A & P and the Needles. The Atlantic & Pacific route was 232 miles shorter, or ten to twelve railroad operating hours. Thus a train via the Atlantic & Pacific would reach San Francisco almost a full day ahead of a train via the Deming line. The Southern Pacific contended this would ruin its passenger traffic. By October 11 the two parties reached agreement and through Pullman sleepers were planned from St. Louis and Kansas City to San Francisco by way of the Atlantic & Pacific, with transfer to the Southern Pacific at the Needles. The Southern Pacific pledged

13

The odd bowl-shaped spark arrestor atop the stack was not standard equipment when Baldwin built this 4-6-0 in 1886. At the Needles, the engine crew pose for a trackside portrait beside No. 51. On the right, it's departure time for the eastbound *Overland Limited*, link 'n pinned behind a Pittsburgh 4-6-0. The depot in the background is the original the Needles station used jointly with the Southern Pacific.

Branded with the Baldwin wagon-top boiler and Santa Fe style pilot, Atlantic & Pacific No. 115 pauses beside the Needles coal chutes to form this 1893 setting. (BE-LOW) the freight crew of No. 71, a sleek 4-6-0 from the Pittsburgh Works, gather for a photograph in the Needles yard.

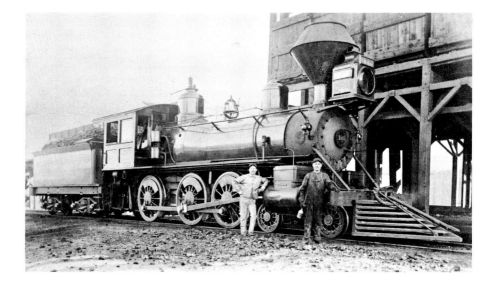

to favor the A & P line for passenger service, rather than its slower Deming line.

On October 18, 1883, General Superintendent W. F. Smith of the Atlantic & Pacific told the correspondent from Railway Age Magazine, "It is with pleasure that I announce the opening of this, the 'All the Year' route for through business on October 21st, in connection with the St. Louis & San Francisco; the Atchison, Topeka & Santa Fe; and the Southern Pacific railroads. Thus forming one of the shortest and best routes between the Mississippi and Missouri rivers on the east and the Pacific Ocean on the west."

The connection with the Southern Pacific at the Needles proved disappointing. Local business of the new road was trifling and the Southern Pacific diverted most of its freight traffic via Ogden or El Paso. Southern Pacific's rush in building the Mojave to the Needles line to bar the Atlantic & Pacific from entering California had done the job. Various courses were open to the Santa Fe. One was to endure the existing state of things, retain the property by keeping the road solvent and pocket the loss. Another course was to give up the enterprise altogether, renounce the idea of ever reaching the Pacific and to leave the road to its creditors and eventual purchase by the Southern Pacific. A third course was to parallel the Southern Pacific by build-

ing an entirely new line from the Needles to San Francisco, a distance of over 600 miles. Such a plan, though physically possible, was financially impracticable. The only remaining course, and the only one really available was the one adopted— the purchase of the Southern Pacific line between the Needles and Mojave on such terms as to secure for the Atlantic & Pacific a practically independent right of way beyond Mojave to Oakland and San Francisco.

After prolonged negotiations, the end was at length accomplished. The results were embodied in four instruments dated August 20, 1884. By these instruments the Atlantic & Pacific bought the Southern Pacific trackage between the Needles and Mojave, 242 miles of railroad for $30,000 per mile, and until the mortgage could be discharged it took an annual lease at six per cent interest. Also the Atlantic & Pacific secured trackage, traffic and facility rights between Mojave, Oakland and San Francisco, as well as terminals at these points, by paying a rental of $1,200 per mile. A complete view of the situation cannot be had without going back a few years. The Southern Pacific was not giving away all of this out of kindness when it faced competition in its empire of California.

Several years before the connection with the Atlantic & Pacific, men of the Santa Fe had their

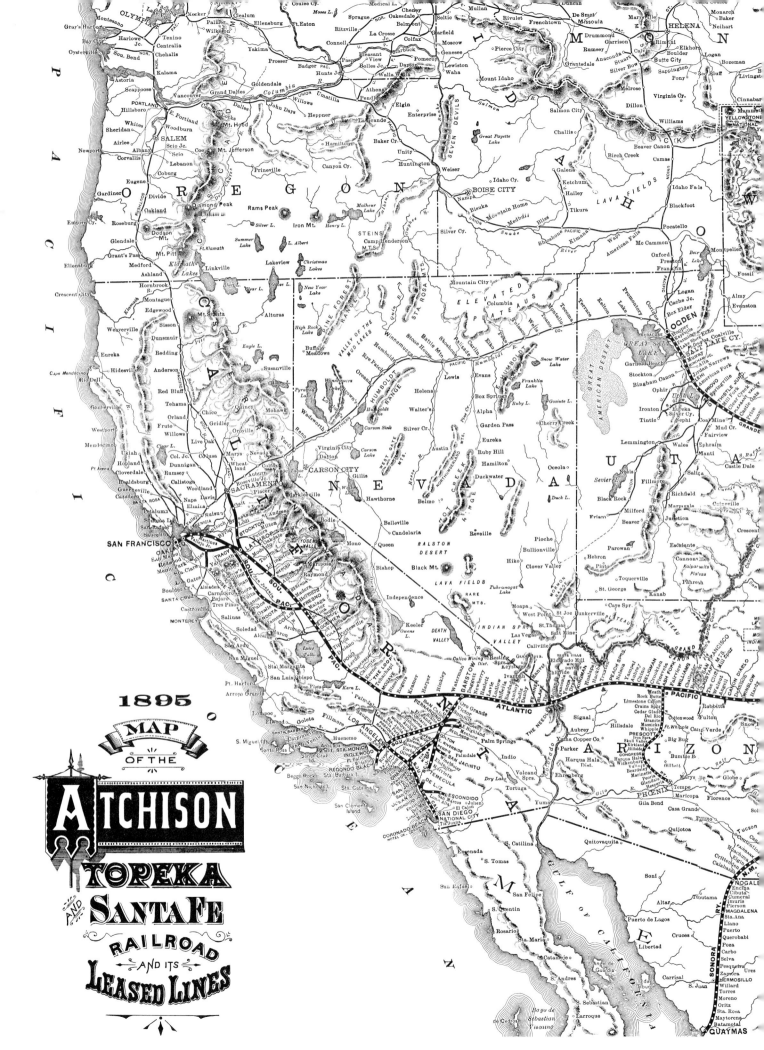

1895 MAP OF THE ATCHISON TOPEKA AND SANTA FE RAILROAD AND ITS LEASED LINES

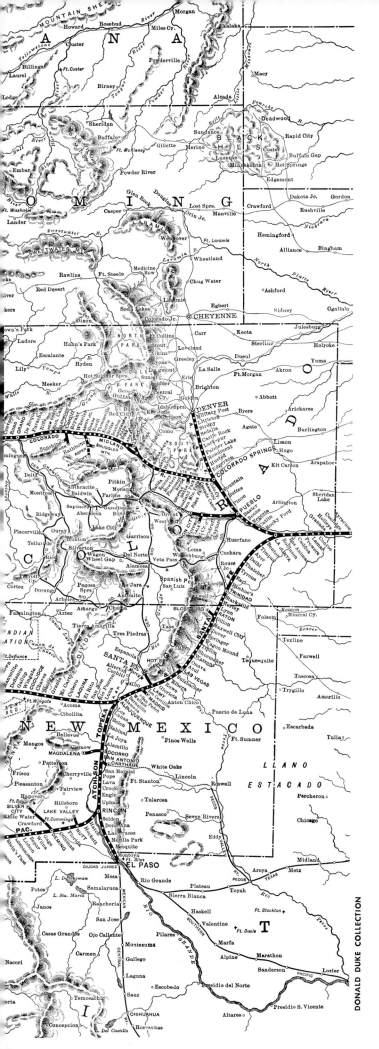

eyes on Mexico. Survey parties had been dispatched to find a line down into the neighbor republic to a natural port on the Pacific. However, the contemplated hook-up with the Atlantic & Pacific route held precedence. In order for an American company to build a railroad in a foreign country the charter had to be changed. In the Massachusetts legislature on March 28, 1879, a bill was introduced. It was submitted by a Mr. Osgood of Salem, who stated that "It was for the benefit of the Atchison, Topeka & Santa Fe Railroad, which proposes to extend its road into Mexican territory. The corporators of the road are largely Massachusetts men, and wish the authority of their own state given to the act of incorporation permitting them to build in a foreign country, which is demanded by the Mexican government before the road can be built." The bill was thus passed and the Santa Fe had the right to extend into Mexico.

A land grant was obtained from the Mexican government to build a railroad through the valley of the Sonora, extending north from Guaymas on the Gulf of California to the borders of the United States and Mexico. On June 20, 1879, the New York Times had this to say: "The Santa Fe Railroad has received the Sonora land grant which the Southern Pacific so much coveted, and which, though it gives 15,000 acres of land to the mile, is of even greater moment to the Southern Pacific, for its passing to another railroad brings a much dreaded rival line to contest the business of the entire Pacific Coast. The grant was originally from El Paso, on the Rio Grande River, the proposed junction of the Southern Pacific and Texas Pacific roads, and then on to Guaymas on the Gulf of California, 350 miles above where the gulf empties into the Pacific Ocean and about the same distance from Mazatlan. The line of the Santa Fe road leaves the Rio Grande and diverges southward from a point just below Polmos and 110 miles above El Paso. Thence it continues to this place, which is 116 miles from the river. Making this the point of divergence from Guaymas, the general southwest bearing is preserved direct to the coast, and the distance from New York is less by 200 miles than by way of El Paso and the Southern Pacific." The article went on to say, "An American railroad traversing Mexican soil must prove an entering wedge

17

The California Southern was the predecessor of the Santa Fe in California. It built from National City to Colton in 1881-82. Baldwin delivered coal burner No. 14 to the California Southern in 1887. Yard men inspect the new beauty on its arrival at National City. At the foot of Front Street in San Diego, No. 3, a four-wheel locomotive shown below works the bay front about 1882. While on the right, the California Southern depot, a showplace in San Diego for many a year. Constructed during 1887-88 along Victorian-Gothic architecture, it was replaced in 1915 by the present station.

to commerce with Mexico, not as now, on a pica-yune scale, but broad and comprehensive. Aside from this, Guaymas is an average distance of 800 miles nearer the principal ports of China than is San Francisco, and upward of 1,000 miles nearer Australia. The Atchison, Topeka & Santa Fe Railroad is backed by unlimited capital, and having a line to the coast not only offering so much the shortest routes, but suffering no hindrance from snow during the winter, will prove a mean competitor to the Southern Pacific who controls not only all the railroads of California, but great steamship lines as well. The command of the company is law on the Pacific Coast."

This was the card the Santa Fe needed and played with a stacked deck the whole way. The Sonora Railway was launched during the summer of 1879, on the Gulf of California, at the port town of Guaymas. By mid-October the rails were completed to Nogales on the Arizona border. Here the new rail-

road joined the tracks of the New Mexico & Arizona Railroad, a Santa Fe subsidiary, and now Santa Fe rails reached from Topeka to the waters of the blue Pacific. Traffic over the line was slight. However, it was the first railroad into Mexico, and had prior rights to all Mexico from the north which the Southern Pacific craved. Huntington feared such expansion by the Santa Fe would eventually destroy all extensions of the Southern Pacific. In exchange for the line from Benson, Arizona, to Guaymas, Mexico, the Southern Pacific surrendered its stranglehold on California. What harm could the Santa Fe do to the Southern Pacific which was so firmly entrenched everywhere in California?

Meanwhile, at the southwest tip of California, lay the town of San Diego. There was a natural land-locked harbor and the perfect spot to serve as a western terminal for a railroad line. Since 1845 the citizens of San Diego had sent representatives east to expound the merits of their city. Six times the San

California Southern No. 3 shifts passenger equipment at National City. The letterboard on the last coach reads *Atchison Topeka & Santa Fe* and was the through coach to Los Angeles established in late 1885.

A brace of 4-4-0's shown above, move an eastbound freight across the San Luis Rey River north of Oceanside during 1886. On the left, a local passenger train crosses a high bridge in Linda Vista Canyon, north of San Diego.

21

Diegans had been promised a railroad. All efforts ended in promises of surveys and projections, yet no rail was ever laid. During 1878, San Diego sent an appeal to Jay Gould to build a line down to San Diego from anywhere. Gould's telegram read, "I don't build railroads, I buy them." The Santa Fe, still building west from Albuquerque under the Atlantic & Pacific charter, was approached as a likely prospect to enjoy the San Diego harbor. The Santa Fe did not overlook any port on the Pacific which showed promise. Financial aid and assistance was given the San Diegans in order that they might project their own independent railroad to meet them at the Colorado River crossing.

The Citizens Railroad Committee of San Diego agreed to form a syndicate to build a railroad to meet the Atlantic & Pacific somewhere in California. Articles of incorporation for the California Southern Railroad Company were drawn in 1881. Shops, a roundhouse and yards were to be built at National City, just on the outskirts of San Diego. Here a wharf

was built for the unloading of rails and other construction equipment. Bridge construction, grading and laying of rails started immediately. The route headed north, paralleling the coast line to San Luis Rey River, site of present-day Oceanside. Thence it turned northeast, following the Santa Margarita River through Temecula Canyon, then north to San Bernardino. This route was shortest to a transcontinental connection and more direct than if it had followed the coast line to the pueblo of Los Angeles.

The Santa Fe survey crews failed to understand the dry Southern California streams which during some parts of the year would swell into a roaring torrent of water, rock and mud. Warned by the early settlers of this condition, the surveyors nevertheless continued up the canyon of the Temecula. Grading in the upper canyon revealed seven miles of solid rock and perpendicular canyon walls. Grades were 150 feet to the mile and the line crossed and recrossed the stream on low trestles. Hundreds of Chinese were brought in to do the grading work

Oceanside, built upon a high bluff, consisted of a few homes, freight shed, siding and Mission San Luis Rey four miles to the east in 1884. On the left, before entering the deep of Temecula Canyon, an 1884 vintage train pauses for water near Fallbrook. Grading the California Southern in Temecula Canyon was a herculean task as evidenced in the view on the right. For nearly seven miles, the track crossed and recrossed the Santa Margarita River through solid rock and perpendicular cliffs. After several complete washouts, the line was abandoned.

V. B. WESTFALL

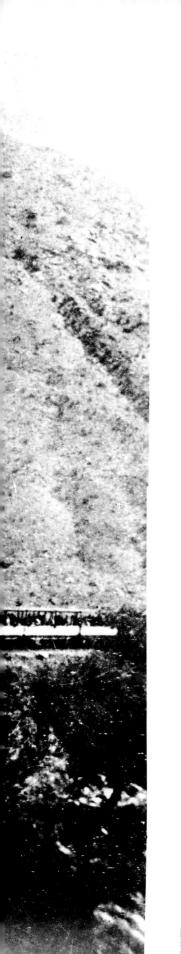

The cliffs of Temecula Canyon were precipitous and imposing to the inspection party as they view the new line in 1882. The big curve shown below was laid in the Santa Margarita River bottom, also subject to washouts. On the left, one of many excursion trains which ran through Temecula Canyon. The locomotives, Nos. 12 and 2 respectively, were Rhode Island 4-4-0 type, built in early 1880's.

The first California Southern train into San Bernardino was decorated with evergreens, flowers and stalks of corn. Squash was piled on the locomotive pilot and ivy around the oil headlight. In the haste to complete the link, the track lacked proper ballast. (BELOW) the busiest building in Perris during 1889 was the Santa Fe depot. The town laid out in 1886 was named for Fred T. Perris, chief engineer of the California Southern. In the upper right, the tracks ran north from Temecula Canyon to Elsinore on an easy grade along the shores of Big Laguna Lake. Elsinore later became a tourist colony.

when the local farmers refused to assist a fool's errand. As the line reached Elsinore, then known as Big Laguna, the grading moved much faster because of the flatter terrain. Some grading on the roadbed through Box Canyon (Cajon Pass) north of San Bernardino was also well under way. The survey was easy, as it followed near the old Los Angeles & Independence Railway survey to the head of the pass, then turned east. The grading work completed was considered sufficient to hold the pass from any rival railroad which might wish to occupy the pass.

Tracklaying soon outstripped the delivery of rails. The road was opened to Fallbrook station on January 2, 1882, some 67 miles from San Diego. Steel was pushed through Temecula Canyon and service as far as Temecula station began March 27 of the same year. Now 79 miles were in operation. To save money and time, rails by-passed Riverside and Arlington for the time being and were built in a direct line to the town of Colton on the Southern Pacific. The line reached Colton on August 14, 1882, 127 miles from National City, the home base of operations. A track connection was made with the Southern Pacific and the first California Southern timetable listed one train a day in each direction. At last San Diego had a railroad connection with the outside world.

In order to extend the California Southern tracks to San Bernardino and up Cajon Pass, it was neces-

sary to cross the Southern Pacific iron at Colton. Prior to that the California Southern tracks joined the Southern Pacfic, but did not cross it. Permission to cross Southern Pacific tracks at this point was denied by Huntington. A fence was then constructed to keep out all those who would trespass on Southern Pacific property. Workmen on the California Southern were furious and tore down the protective fence as fast as Southern Pacific forces put it up. The Southern Pacific was served with an injunction by the California Southern for a right to cross. The litigation dragged on for months. However, on August 7, 1883, a California Southern crew secretly attempted to put in a crossing frog. After it was in place a Southern Pacific ten-wheeled locomotive bore down on the crew and the engine continuously moved over the location, resting only to permit a mainline train to pass east and west. There was no demonstration of force, but rumors were passed that armed men were riding the engine. This condition remained for three days. Litigation between the California Southern and the Southern Pacific concerning the crossing terminated August 11, when the courts favored the California Southern.

The extension to San Bernardino was quickly completed and the first regular passenger train entered that city on September 13, 1883. The train was decorated with evergreens, flowers and stalks of corn and hundreds of pounds of squash were piled

Rising pillars of steam and oil smoke pile high into the clear California sky in 1896 as California Southern Nos. 66-68-60 triple into Summit after battling mighty Cajon Pass. This eastbound drag freight took three hours to make the 25 mile ascent with three 4-6-0 type locomotives built by the Pittsburgh Works in 1887. (OPPOSITE PAGE) the name *California Limited* is only slightly less old and romantic in railroad legend than the name Santa Fe itself. It was the pride of the line in 1895 as it raced toward Los Angeles a few minutes out of San Bernardino.

on the locomotive pilot. The first link in the Santa Fe Route to the Pacific was completed. A celebration was held in San Bernardino that was remembered for years.

Huntington took a dim view of the fast progress the California Southern was making. He knew the Atlantic & Pacific was not happy with the situation at the Needles and that something would happen. He feared most of all the duplication of trackage between the Needles and the California Southern. Huntington was being pushed from two sides now and his California domain was slowly coming to an end.

Preparations for the continuation of the California Southern through Cajon Pass were taking shape in January 1884. It was not decided where the California Southern would meet the Atlantic & Pacific. President Strong of the Santa Fe asked the California Southern to hold up construction until the Southern Pacific came to terms. While conversations were being passed the storm hit. The winter of 1883-1884 was the wettest on record. More than 40 inches of rain fell during a four-week period. The line through Temecula Canyon was inundated with walls of water and completely washed out.

Eight of the twelve miles of roadbed had gone to sea. Bridge timbers were found down along the coast for more than 80 miles. A passenger train had been stranded in a section of the canyon and it took railroad officials three weeks before they reached the stricken train. Luckily a local farm provided enough food to keep the passengers and crew alive until the rescue party could reach them. It was estimated that it would cost $250,000 to restore the line. The California Southern was near bankruptcy. The farmers shouted, "We told you so!"

The Santa Fe immediately came to the rescue and agreed to an exchange of bonds. New rails were shipped in and hundreds of Chinese were put to work in clearing a shelf in Temecula Canyon for a roadbed. In the meantime the agreement for lease of the Needles to Mojave section had been reached with the Southern Pacific and the Santa Fe had its gateway to California.

Trains of the California Southern began running through Temecula Canyon on January 6, 1885, and all the Chinese were immediately transferred to Cajon Pass. Further surveys were made, the final one producing a maximum grade slightly less than 185 feet to the mile. It would be a rugged pull for

SANTA FE RAILWAY

The branch line to Escondido was built in 1887 as the California Central Railroad Company. The tracks left the mainline at Oceanside, headed east and up a rich fertile valley to the foot of Palomar Mountain. The view above shows the daily mixed train beside the Santa Fe depot with the town of Escondido in the background. (BELOW) The Santa Fe No. 646 built by Manchester in 1887. This clean coal burner was former Southern California Railway No. 15. The shops, engine terminal and yards of the California Southern are shown in the upper right as they were originally built at National City in 1881. By 1887, when this view was made, major repair facilities had moved to San Bernardino. In the lower right, the twice weekly mixed to Temecula pauses at Elsinore in 1905 behind Santa Fe No. 10.

the small engines of the time, but no other course could be taken except by a tunnel. This was not feasible because of the San Andreas fault which edges Cajon Pass; one earthquake would crumble any tunnel. The old Los Angeles & Independence which started a tunnel through Cajon years before, had given up the idea as a lost cause. Santa Fe rails were then pushed from Waterman, as Barstow was then called, and from San Bernardino. A final spike was driven in the pass on November 9, 1885, marking the completion of the final link in the Santa Fe Route to the Pacific. The first train over the completed line on November 12 was a freight with eight loads of rail for the Riverside branch.

Along with official announcement of the last spike, word was passed along that agreements had been made with the Southern Pacific for joint use of the Southern Pacific mainline tracks between Colton and Los Angeles at a rental of $1,200 per mile a year. This agreement became effective November 29, 1885, and through service between Los Angeles and San Diego via Colton was established. Locomotive No. 354 of the Santa Fe pulled the first train into Los Angeles. San Diego was now on the map and its citizens could travel across the United States by rail.

A fierce rate war started in earnest between the two rival railroads. The Santa Fe served notice that it was dropping all association with the Transcontinental Traffic Association when that association failed to distribute the existing traffic equally. The Santa Fe felt it could handle more volume than it was getting and was entitled to more. A passenger ticket from Missouri to Los Angeles costing $125 in 1885 was reduced to $15 and at the last went down to an even dollar. Many from the farm belt pulled up stakes and moved to California to start a new life. Kansas, Iowa and Indiana were the states heavily hit. Immigrants also poured into Southern California on the cheap rate to have a look at the so-called paradise.

Everything was ripe in Southern California for a boom. Wages were high, work plentiful, and the mild weather provided the frosting on the big cake. Fruit and vegetables were growing in the fine rich soil. Shipping costs due to the freight rate war were also low, money was easy to borrow. Midwestern real estate agents had a field day setting up new towns and enticing the Iowa farmer to give up his land and move to Southern California. During the spring of 1887, thirteen new townsites were staked out between Los Angeles and San Bernardino. Dur-

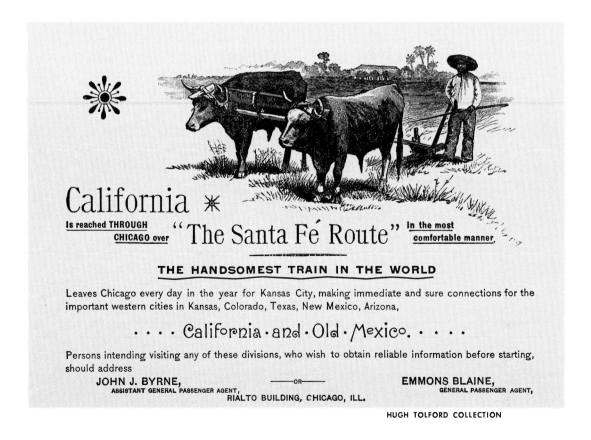

California ✳
Is reached THROUGH CHICAGO over "The Santa Fé Route" In the most comfortable manner.

THE HANDSOMEST TRAIN IN THE WORLD

Leaves Chicago every day in the year for Kansas City, making immediate and sure connections for the important western cities in Kansas, Colorado, Texas, New Mexico, Arizona,

· · · · California · and · Old · Mexico. · · · ·

Persons intending visiting any of these divisions, who wish to obtain reliable information before starting, should address

JOHN J. BYRNE,
ASSISTANT GENERAL PASSENGER AGENT,
——OR——
EMMONS BLAINE,
GENERAL PASSENGER AGENT,
RIALTO BUILDING, CHICAGO, ILL.

HUGH TOLFORD COLLECTION

GRAND FREE EXCURSION AND FREE LUNCH
— TO —
GARVANZO!

FRIDAY, MAY 6, 1887.

Train leaves L. A. & S. G. V. R. R. Depot at 9:30 A. M.

Auction Sale at 10 o'clock A. M.

Don't fail to examine the Business and Residence Lots in the healthful town of Garvanzo. Only four and one half miles from Los Angeles, on the line of the L. A. & S. G. V. R. R.—has five trains daily each way.

The A. T. & S. F. R. R. will have completed their Connection at Garvanzo by June 1st.

Water is piped to this property from the Mountain Water Company, and charged for at the Los Angeles City water rates.

This Sale is Peremptory, and it is to the interest of all persons desiring good investments to be in attendance at this sale.

For Further information apply to

ROGERS, BOOTH & CO.

134 North Main Street, Los Angeles,

OR ON THE GROUNDS AT GARVANZO.

NEWHALL'S SONS & CO., Auctioneers,

225 & 227 BUSH STREET, SAN FRANCISCO.

The land boom roared into high gear by 1887. The Los Angeles & San Gabriel Valley Railroad was the first of the steam suburban roads built during this period. Under the guidance of S. P. Jewett, a young engineer from Chicago, a line was constructed from Los Angeles to Pasadena, and to as many communities east as traffic would warrant. A free train ride and free lunch lured land speculators to Garvanzo, a real estate promotion midway between Los Angeles and Pasadena. In the scene below, the local passenger pauses on the Arroyo Seco trestle at Garvanzo for a photograph. The region was later named Highland Park and became part of the City of Los Angeles.

ing 1889 the bubble burst and many lost everything they owned, but out of it all came thousands of acres of flourishing farms, beautiful orange groves and foothills full of prosperous towns.

As a result of the great boom, the Santa Fe realized that trackage rights over the Southern Pacific were not profitable. Its own rails into Los Angeles were needed. The charter of the California Southern did not permit construction of branch lines, but no stipulation was made against leased lines or feeder lines built by dummy corporations. The first line to be purchased was the Los Angeles & San Gabriel Valley Railroad Company. The acquisition was completed in 1887 and formed a link in the San Bernardino & Los Angeles Railway Company which was formed in November 1886, to build from San Bernardino west to a junction with the Los Angeles & San Gabriel Valley Railroad, some 40 miles away. The Los Angeles & San Gabriel Valley Railroad ran from Los Angeles to Pasadena via Highland Park and extended eastward to Lamanda Park and proposed to build farther into the San Gabriel Valley. The total length of the line was approximately 26 miles and was first opened to service on September 16, 1885.

The two railroads consolidated officially on June 1, 1887, as a part of the California Central. Rails were joined together at Mud Springs on May 20, 1887, at which time the first train was run through to San Bernardino. All locomotives and cars of the

The first locomotive on the Los Angeles & San Gabriel Valley Railroad was a second-hand 4-4-0 with inclined cylinders—typical of the Civil War era. (BELOW) the line was officially opened September 16, 1885, when No. 2 with coaches and open cars pulled into Pasadena all decorated in streamers, bunting and American flags. The Los Angeles & San Gabriel Valley Railroad presented to Walter Raymond 25 acres of land on Beach Hill, south of Pasadena. Here Raymond erected a hotel of colossal proportions. It became known as one of the finest winter hotels in America. A stylish depot was built at the base of the hill which was re-named Raymond Hill. At the upper left, a train pauses beside Raymond Station. Note Raymond jitney and the Alhambra & Pasadena Railway horsecar. In the lower left, the Raymond Hotel and the railroad during the winter of 1894-95.

California Southern and Santa Fe were transferred from the Southern Pacific yards at Los Angeles to a new depot built at the foot of First Street in Los Angeles. By the first of June, all trains arrived and departed from this new station and did so for many years.

Additional branches were added to the ever-growing network of Santa Fe rails in and around Los Angeles. The Riverside, Santa Ana & Los Angeles Railway Company was incorporated September 29, 1885, to build down the Santa Ana canyon, then north and west to Los Angeles. Tracks were extended from Riverside, south to the townsite of Orange. Tracks were completed to Santa Ana during September 1887, and pushed on into Los Angeles via Fullerton during August 1888. This became a second main line or loop for the Santa Fe between Los Angeles and San Bernardino.

A branch was extended to Redondo where the Santa Fe made an effort to build a small harbor for ocean vessels. The Southern Pacific was building a long wharf north of Santa Monica called the Port of Los Angeles and it seemed more logical than Redondo. The Los Angeles & Santa Monica Railway Company was organized January 6, 1886, to build from Los Angeles to Port Ballona. Here the Santa Fe long wharf was built connecting it with Los Angeles via Inglewood, a distance of seventeen miles. Port Ballona was used for several years by lumber ships, but not enough trade passed through the port to keep it in operation.

The Santa Fe began construction of a "Surf Line" between Los Angeles and San Diego to avoid any further recurring washouts in Temecula Canyon. The San Bernardino & San Diego Railway Company was incorporated November 20, 1886, to build south from Santa Ana to San Juan Capistrano near the coast, then down along the coast to meet the present California Southern mainline just north of Oceanside. With the completion of the "Surf

Big hotels labeled Pasadena as a land of relaxation for the eastern nabob. The Green Hotel was one of Pasadena's finest caravansaries, blending Spanish and Moorish architecture with beautiful gardens surrounding the hotel and Santa Fe depot. Ladies without escorts might board the Pullman compartment cars of the *California Limited* by walking from the hotel to trainside through the gardens as shown above. On the right, the stylish ten-wheeler standing at Pasadena's depot on a summer evening with train No. 8, the *Overland Express*, with Pullmans and mail for Chicago. Mail and baggage wagons on the left fill the depot parking lot in the era before motor cars.

DONALD DUKE COLLECTION

Far and away the most popular social event on Saturday, July 29, 1893, was the formal opening of the new Santa Fe *La Grande* station. Los Angeles gentry either rode the new electric cars of the Los Angeles Consolidated Electric Railway to the event or came by carriage, hitching them in front of the big edifice. As the afternoon progressed, the crowd gathered in the passageway under the big sign *Santa Fe Route* to hear the eloquent remarks of Governor Eli Murray and Senator White. The photograph in the upper left illustrates this historic event. Fire had destroyed the original Los Angeles station in 1887. It became necessary to build a permanent station for the growing metropolis. A 27-year old draftsman in the engineering department by the name of Frank Levet was assigned the task of designing the new station. Construction began during 1891 on the architecturally unique brick structure of Turkish and Moorish design. Standing on Santa Fe Avenue between First and Second Street, the station and tracks were along the west bank of the Los Angeles River in downtown Los Angeles. An aerial view of the station layout is presented above. The interior included a trim of Oregon pine and California Redwood, with separate lunchrooms and waiting rooms for ladies and gentlemen. The motto *East or West, Santa Fe is Best*, was carved in sandstone in each waiting room. A small park adjoining the station was complete with swaying palms and California poppies. The canopy over the tracks protected the ladies from winter exposure as they boarded the *California Limited* or one of fifty-two trains arriving and departing daily. *La Grande* was the favorite spot for the movie colony. Often the station signs were covered by one reading "Warm Springs" or some fictional town. Many movie queens were caught on celluloid as they waved from the rear platform of a departing train or boarding a Pullman with fanfare. The local passenger train on the left blasts its rhythmic exhaust as it pulls out of *La Grande* on the famous *Kite Route* trip. This run was a favorite Sunday excursion that made a figure eight with San Bernardino in the center. With the opening of new Union Passenger Terminal in 1939, old *La Grande* saw its last passenger train after 46 years of faithful service. The station was used as extra office space for several years until razed in 1946 to make way for a freight depot.

39

PARK

40

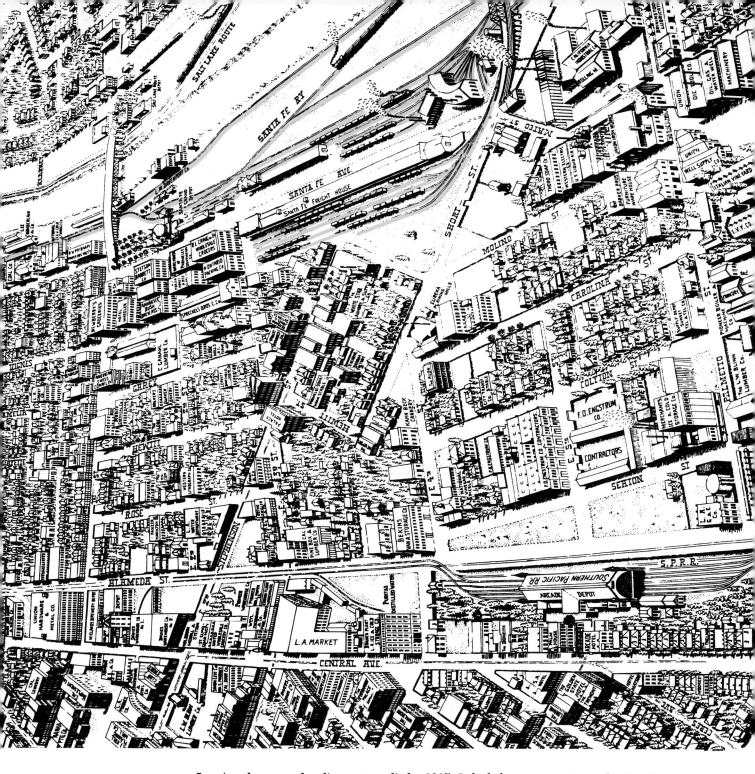

Los Angeles was a bustling metropolis by 1905. It had three transcontinental railroads and three separate railroad stations. The pictorial map shown above pinpoints the railroad stations in relation to the downtown section of Los Angeles which is off the map on the left. The Santa Fe facilities are located on the west bank of the Los Angeles River. The Redondo Junction roundhouse is located on the lower right. Above the roundhouse is the freight house and *La Grande* station. The line to San Diego and San Bernardino via Fullerton leaves the map on the lower right by the roundhouse. The line east via Pasadena follows the west bank of the river, then crossing by the foothills of Elysian Park. The Southern Pacific Arcade depot can be found in the lower left hand corner. The Salt Lake Route station is directly across the river from *La Grande*.

The Surf Line ran from Los Angeles to San Diego, a distance of 126 miles, passing through rich oil fields, garden farms and miles of the most extensive citrus groves in California. At Capistrano, the line passed near Mission San Juan Capistrano, famous for the swallows which return yearly on St. Joseph's Day (March 19). In the scene above, a group of tourists board a local at the mission style depot. The serpentine tracks reach the coast at Capistrano Beach and edged the ocean along the barren coastline, passing occasional seaside resort towns and south to San Diego. Delmar and the Stratford Inn on the hill above the depot was a popular seaside resort as shown in the upper left. (LOWER LEFT) The wide, sandy beaches and high precipitous cliffs of San Clemente were also a must on the tourist ticket.

Line" on August 12, 1888, the rail distance between Los Angeles and San Diego was shortened considerably. The Temecula line was kept in operation, but was no longer considered as the mainline.

Lines such as the San Diego Central Railroad Company, the San Bernardino Valley Railway Company and the San Jacinto Valley Railway Company were organized to build branch lines into the rich agricultural areas. The California Central Railway Company was organized May 1887, to bring all the associated lines under one corporate structure. The California Central had no motive power of its own, but depended on the California Southern. Along with the reorganization, the main shops were moved from National City to San Bernardino which was more centrally located. The main offices of the California Southern were moved from San Diego to Los Angeles about the same time. Another shake-up in management came in 1889. The California Southern, Redondo Beach Railway Company and all the California Central properties were consolidated into the Southern California Railway Company. This

Redondo was 22 miles southwest of Los Angeles on the Santa Fe. The eminent architectural feature of Redondo was its handsome hotel, erected on a high terrace with magnificent visual sweep of the sea. Being an annual resort, many tourists came from the bleak east by train to taste the salt spray and bask in the winter sun. In the view above, one of the daily trains pauses along the sandy beach with the Redondo Hotel in the background. The view on the left was taken from the long wharf where steamers of the Pacific Coast Steamship Company docked. Redondo also held commercial importance as a lumber and merchandise port.

Spectators from all over California poured into Escondido during 1910 to bid on the rich farm land that was auctioned off on the station platform. (BELOW) When the local paused for its photograph at Carlsbad station, sometime around the turn of the century, all the crew gathered beside the hefty 4-4-0 except the express messenger.

new operating carrier was a consolidation of all Santa Fe interests in the Southern California region. Eventually all motive power assigned to the Southern California Railway was renumbered into its own system. The Southern California Railway was leased to the Santa Fe June 1, 1904, and by January 17, 1906, it was sold to the Santa Fe. Thus ended the various ownerships of the Southern California lines.

By 1889, the Santa Fe network comprised 8,118 miles including the lines which it owned jointly to the extent of 50 per cent with other companies. With the hub now in Chicago instead of Boston, its extremities rested in Galveston, San Diego, Los Angeles and Chicago. The Santa Fe strength began to drop as other railroads penetrated the stronghold. Economic conditions began to drop too, and so did the revenues of the Santa Fe. British banks, holding the majority of the bonds and the reins of the enterprise, compelled President Strong to retire. Unfortunately, it was too late; the canker had eaten more deeply into the system than anticipated, and at last the British interests refused to advance another penny of credit. Bankruptcy was staved for a time, but the end was inevitable. The crash came in 1893. The Santa Fe, comprising 8,118 miles, went down with a debt unheard of in financial circles.

For two years the property remained in the receiver's hands, when a reorganization committee was appointed by the representatives of interests in New York and London. Their deliberations culminated in the creation of a new company under the title "The Atchison, Topeka & Santa Fe Railway"; the only change was the substitution of the word railway for railroad. The new company took over the property of the old company, with the exception of what had been sold by the receivers, and Edward Payson Ripley was elected to guide the future destinies.

President Ripley was a strong man of quick decision, keen imagination and great acuteness. An estimate of his administrative powers may be gathered from the fact that he held the reins of the Santa Fe for 24 years during which he completely rehabilitated the system. When Ripley settled down to his task, he quickly laid his finger upon the weak spots. Many small lines which he found to be eating into profits were sold, abandoned or torn up. He

SOUTHERN CALIFORNIA RAILWAY

SANTA FE ROUTE

PASSENGER TRAIN SCHEDULES

In effect February 23rd, 1896.

ISSUE OF FEBRUARY 23RD, 1896.

NOTICE—The Time Tables herein show the time at which trains may be expected to arrive at and depart from the several stations, but their arrival and departure at the time stated is not guaranteed and the Southern California Railway Company reserves the right to vary from the same at pleasure and without notice. Where time is not shown trains do not stop.

K. H. WADE, General Manager..................Los Angeles, Cal.
JNO. J. BYRNE, Gen'l Pass. Agent...............Los Angeles, Cal.
H. K. GREGORY Ass't Gen'l Pass. Agt ....Los Angeles, Cal.

10M. 2-22-96.

The Santa Fe trademark used on the above timetable employed the British lion in respect for the early financial assistance in the building of the railroad to California.

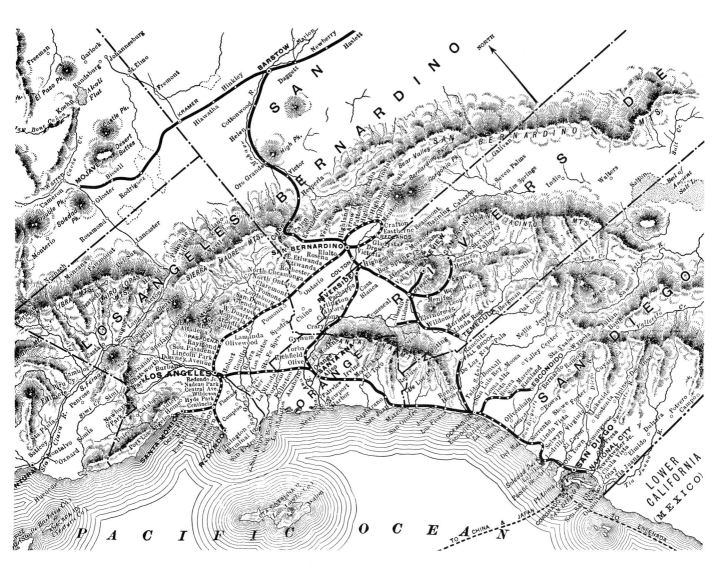

By 1899, the Santa Fe rails reached the more popu-
lous regions of Southern California. The old line
through Temecula Canyon was abandoned thus
forming two branch lines from the break. Now the
Surf Line was the mainline to San Diego. A line
to Santa Monica had been completed to connect
with the Southern Pacific long wharf which was the
Port of Los Angeles for a time.

discovered the holdings in the St. Louis & San Francisco Railway Company to be of such doubtful value
that they were sold. Another elaborate overhaul
was that of the Atlantic & Pacific Railroad across
New Mexico and Arizona, of which the Santa Fe
secured at a foreclosure sale full ownership from
the St. Louis & San Francisco Railway Company.

In his reorganization he proved remarkably far-
sighted. He disapproved of any holdings in the
Sonora Railway running into Mexico. He rushed to
completion the transfer of ownership of this property in full exchange for the Needles to Mojave line.
The mainline between Chicago and Los Angles was
given a complete engineering overhaul and shortened some 50 miles. As a result of these wise moves
the steel highway under Ripley developed into a
gridiron of 11,706 miles with more than 4,000 miles
of sidings. Santa Fe thus became the first class trans-

Many years ago during the rainy seasons, traffic on Cajon Pass was interrupted by large land slides. The earthen sides of deep cuts, softened by the torrents poured down on the tracks. A former Santa Fe official overcame this difficulty by an ingenious contrivance, consisting of a series of roofed terraces on the sides, arranged laterally with the track so as to carry away the water to the ends of the cut. This region became known as Terras Cut to the railroad men. Even today it is called Terras Cut, however with modern machinery the walls have been cut back. In the lower view, the *Overland Express* approaches Summit, atop Cajon Pass.

48

The Santa Fe rails reached the rich gold deposits of the Mojave desert in the early 1900's. On the left, a quaint 2-8-0 chugs up the long grade and around the big loop that led to the smelter at Searchlight. (BELOW) The Johannesburg station on the Rands-burg Branch. This line was leased from the Rands-burg Railway in 1903. Today the mines are gone and the handiwork of man has been left to the raw desert. The lower view shows the Barstow depot and Harvey House after its completion.

continental mainline that Colonel Cyrus K. Holliday had envisioned.

The first major expansion of the revitalized Santa Fe was the purchase of the stock of the incomplete San Francisco & San Joaquin Valley Railway. Arrangements were made in December, 1898, and final purchase was formally concluded November 1, 1899. During the intervening months the completion of the line was vigorously pushed, the unfinished portion being between Stockton and Point Richmond, opposite San Francisco on the bay. In addition to securing a long-sought entrance to San Francisco and branch lines in the rich San Joaquin Valley, the

Santa Fe gained another valuable asset in the person of William B. Storey, Jr. He had directed the construction of the valley road from the very first and now, under the Santa Fe flag, advanced rapidly up the official ladder. In fact, he had such administrative powers that he followed Ripley as president of the entire Santa Fe Railway.

Cracking the monopoly of the Southern Pacific in the rich San Joaquin Valley was an even more formidable task than breaking the Huntington wall at the Needles. Santa Fe is unable to claim major credit for this victory. The valley shippers refused to wear the yoke of the Southern Pacific and waged

Riverside was an arid, dreary wasteland in 1870 when the Southern California Colony Association started building the upper canal of the Santa Ana River. When the canal reached the settlement in 1871, the colony was named Riverside. By December 1885, rails of the California Southern reached Riverside by following the water level grade of the canal. The illustration below was taken about 1897 with locomotive No. 1 and a combination coach pulled beside the old depot.

war against Huntington by organizing the "people's railroad." Widespread dissatisfaction with the Southern Pacific showed itself in persistent complaints against local freight rates held to be highly discriminatory in character. The monopolisitc tendencies of the powerful corporation and its alleged domination over the political life of California were hard to fight. Shippers claimed that a car to New York could be sent cheaper than from the same shipping point to Bakersfield or even San Francisco. Many charged that pack animals were cheaper than the Southern Pacific and pack trains were often seen working between towns of the San Joaquin Valley served by Southern Pacific rails. The only way to fight the Southern Pacific at its own game was to build another railroad down the San Joaquin Valley and connect with the new Santa Fe.

In June 1893, a committee of shippers was appointed to solicit subscriptions for the San Francisco & San Joaquin Valley Railroad. The line would begin at Stockton, then proceed due south to a point in Kern County (Bakersfield). Passengers and freight destined for San Francisco and other bay region ports would be transferred at Stockton to a steamer. Subscriptions were few at first, many fearing the long arm of the Southern Pacific. Another meeting of the committee was held during January, 1895, and it was decided that once and for all the railroad was to be built or the idea given up completely. All agreed the railroad was sorely needed, but the money required kept voices weak. The success of the meeting can be credited to Claus Spreckels, leading sugar refiner on the Pacific Coast, who subscribed half a million dollars, augmented by a hundred thousand from each of his sons, John D. and Rudolph. This brought swift changes to the complexion of the whole enterprise. Wide publicity was given to the new railroad and large numbers of small and fractional subscriptions came from farmers up and down the San Joaquin Valley. As a result, to employ the words of Professor Stuart Daggett, "It may be said that there has probably never been a commercial enterprise launched on the coast so advertised, praised, and predicted about as was the projected San Francisco & San Joaquin Valley Railroad. Participation in the movement became a test of local patriotism."

Actual construction began at Stockton July 22, 1895, when a shipment of rails and ties arrived by steamer. Grading, bridging and tracklaying moved quite rapidly, as the route was almost water level in many areas. The line was completed from Stockton to Fresno early in October 1896. A mammoth barbecue was held and festivities lasted several days. The occasion was more like a fair than the opening of a new railroad. The celebration marking the completion of the line into Bakersfield took place on May 27, 1898, and a similar scene duplicated the Fresno event.

While the Valley Road failed to fulfill the hopes of its projectors, and while from a purely financial standpoint it did not justify its organization, it may nevertheless be deemed justifiable on the grounds of local rate reductions and subsequent development of the entire San Joaquin Valley. Steps were continually being taken to prevent stock from being purchased by the Southern Pacific or their agents. When the Santa Fe began negotiations for the purchase of the Valley Road, few brows were raised and many shippers looked forward to the eventual sale and another route east. The Santa Fe had given assurance to the owners that the competing line would be preserved at all costs.

The story is told that President Ripley called on Huntington to tell him of the completed sale. Huntington is said to have remarked, "Yes, I knew you had bought it. This is a sad day for me and the Southern Pacific. I had longed for the time when Spreckels would come and beg me to take the white elephant off his hands."

Santa Fe was prepared to build a line of its own over the Tehachapi between Mojave and Kern Junction, if necessary. Realizing this, the Southern Pacific agreed to grant Santa Fe trackage rights over this stretch of 67.38 miles. The terms included station and operating facilities for handling of trains. This agreement was to begin January 16, 1899, and run until cancelled by either party by giving five years' written notice. The Santa Fe agreed to give the Southern Pacific 60 per cent of the revenues from local businss on the joint trackage as rental and payment of $2\frac{1}{4}$ per cent per annum on valuation, plus half the taxes and maintenance of the line.

A momentous event was in the making on October 5, 1896, as the first train on the San Francisco & San Joaquin Valley Railroad made its inaugural run. The decorated train shown above was on the way to Fresno having left Stockton earlier in the day. Completion of the road broke the Southern Pacific stronghold on the rich San Joaquin Valley. The regular train became known as the *Emancipator*. The active stable of San Francisco & San Joaquin Valley steam motive power came from Baldwin. The 65-ton freight locomotive below was built in 1896. On the right, a passenger train clatters across one of the many steel viaducts spanning the deep ravines between Stockton and Richmond. The former SF&SJV locomotive was renumbered to a Santa Fe "0" series number to indicate it was slated for an early retirement.

Completion of the final link between Stockton and Point Richmond involved a series of engineering feats. One was the crossing of the tule swamps between Stockton and the San Joaquin River where from ten to 25 feet of living and dead tule plants were located. Canals were dredged on each side of the proposed right of way for a distance of sixteen miles. As the muck was removed, it was piled high in the middle to form a base of some 100 feet. Clay, rocks and sand were added in alternating layers with the tule plants after water had been drained and a crust formed. Tracks were then laid on top after a firm foundation had been made.

Construction of Franklin Tunnel between Glen Fraser and Christie was another task more difficult than expected. The bore was to be 5,560 feet in length, one of the longest tunnels on the Santa Fe lines. The tunnel was quickly lined with timbers as work progressed in the bore. The surrounding earth contained a great deal of moisture and the earth began to swell. Pressure developed against the heavy timbers, causing them to snap like match sticks. Dampness created extensive rot even before the tunnel was completed. Engineers found no solu-

tion and the opinion was that the bore should be abandoned in favor of a switchback. Storey, who had built the valley section of the line, was called in. He began to drain the water from the mountain with a series of pipes; before long the water ran its course and the ground dried.

A terminal in San Francisco was needed by Santa Fe, but every bayside spot was either taken by the Southern Pacific or some steamship firm. Various steamship concerns were approached regarding a lease agreement. They, however, could not handle the traffic the Santa Fe proposed and reclamation of China Basin, a large mud flat under water at high tide, for a terminal site was the only possible alternative. The Santa Fe Terminal Company was formed to install the necessary facilities at this point. A stone sea wall was built and the basin behind filled with dry earth and rock. Slips and a shed were erected and tracks laid for unloading of cars. At least four million cubic yards of rock and earth were used in this undertaking. The slips sagged several times, then more supports were added and they held firm.

May 1, 1900, found the first freight train making

The powerful little *San Pablo* was a familiar sight on San Francisco Bay between Richmond and the Ferry Building for over 30 years. Although the *Ocean Wave* made history, her light engines could not match the *San Pablo's* 2,000 horsepower. (BELOW) William B. Storey in the dark suit poses for the camera at Stockton in 1902. Storey who built the Valley Line later became president of Santa Fe.

its way over the new line between Stockton and Point Richmond. Passenger service followed on July 1. The Santa Fe ferry *Ocean Wave* left her slip at the foot of Market Street on July 6, to start the first direct Santa Fe service between San Francisco and Chicago. Forty minutes later the *Ocean Wave* pulled into the ferry slip at Old Tiburon, then the Santa Fe terminal. Locomotive No. 250 and a string of polished cars pulled alongside to load the passengers and baggage. The train then charged out of town, up through Franklin Tunnel, over the tule bogs and into Stockton. The last major obstacle had been conquered in a desire to reach San Francisco.

The narrow gauge California & Nevada Railroad was purchased to secure a right of way into Oakland. The road was many miles longer and only

11.32 miles were used in reaching the proposed Oakland terminal. The line from Port Richmond to Oakland was renamed the Oakland & East Side Railroad, the first train rolling over the standard gauge rails on May 16, 1904.

Ripley's program for profitable expansion continued during 1901, when the Santa Fe either purchased or built several short segments of trackage. The Sunset Railway, from Bakersfield to Sunset, was constructed jointly with the Southern Pacific and extensions were continued toward Maricopa and Taft, reaching the rich oil deposits at the right time. The California Eastern was purchased to tap the Ivanpah Valley located in the Mojave desert region. The Randsburg Railway from Kramer to Johannesburg was also purchased to tap the rich gold deposits.

During 1901, the Baldwin Locomotive Works delivered this four-cylinder Vauclain Compound capable of high speed passenger service. The train above prepares to depart Richmond for a fast run down the Valley.

Invasion of the California redwood empire north of San Francisco was the next major expansion move by Ripley and his Santa Fe. The redwood empire was rich in heavy timber and the extensive forests promised huge volumes of finished lumber for waiting eastern markets. Ripley also viewed a through line all the way to Portland, Oregon. The San Francisco & Northwestern Railway was formed to purchase some of the small railroads already built in the redwood region. The Eel River & Eureka Railroad, the California Midland Railroad, the California & Northern Railway, plus the rail lines of the Pacific Lumber Company within Humboldt County, were purchased. Surveys ran south to a connection with the recently acquired Fort Bragg & Southeastern Railroad, then south and east to the Santa Fe mainline at Point Richmond.

The Southern Pacific was not sitting idly by and had no intention to watch Ripley swallow up the entire redwood empire. Harriman now had control of the Southern Pacific and he prepared for battle. Each road grabbed any stretch of track already constructed, whether short line or logging road. Santa Fe and Southern Pacific survey crews often met deep in the redwoods, each trying to locate the best right of way first. It became apparent that duplication of service for the amount of potential business would be next to suicide for either railroad.

Rumors were also floating down from Portland that James J. Hill of the Great Northern planned future extensions into Northern California.

Once again the two railroads met face to face. It was decided to join forces and form a new company called the Northwestern Pacific Railroad Company. It was incorporated on January 8, 1907, with stock in the new enterprise to be equally divided. Nearly 500 miles of track were extended right through the heart of the rich timber territory.

The Santa Fe never was able to successfully integrate the Northwestern Pacific into its system. Lack of a direct connection on its own rails caused delay and heavy costs due to transfer to car ferries or interchange with the Southern Pacific. The Santa Fe half-interest in the Northwestern Pacific was sold in 1929 to the Southern Pacific.

The problems of the Santa Fe were not solved when the transcontinental lines were completed or when its network of branch lines was constructed. There never was a time when it could pause for an idle period of indulgent reflections upon things already done. To survive, it had to improve both property and service; all the more so because of the untold business conditions which faced it.

The Santa Fe was ill-equipped in 1896 to carry out its chosen role. The lean years had scarred the trunk and branches. Equipment had not been main-

The populace of Eureka gather at the San Francisco & Northwestern depot to witness the arrival of the first train. On the left, a Scotia bound train with locomotive No. 3 on the point. The Eureka depot shown below was an impressive structure. The tall tower bearing the Santa Fe crest could be seen for miles around.

Woodburner No. 5 departs Happy Camp of the Holmes Eureka Lumber Co. with a load of logs. (CENTER-RIGHT) The same engine as an oil burner heads across the Eel River trestle near Holmes. (CENTER-LEFT) A group of woodsmen on the way to camp stand beside a Santa Fe coach. (LOWER) The Eel River & Eureka shops and wharf on Humboldt Bay were acquired with the purchase of the line.

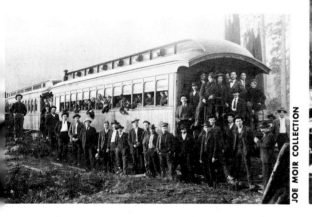

Mighty monarchs of the redwood forest on the way to be processed into lumber behind a former Santa Fe steamer. (BELOW) With locomotive No. 136, a handsome 4-6-0 on its drawbar, the Eureka bound passenger snakes its way through magnificent stands of giant redwoods along the banks of the Eel River. (UPPER LEFT) Avenue of Giants—yielding only to passing Northwestern Pacific trains or the sun streaming through the dense foliage. (LOWER LEFT) A pastoral interlude at Fortuna as the local pulls into town behind a Baldwin 4-4-0 from the Santa Fe stable.

tained and was obsolete. Locomotives were light and the passenger equipment lacked modern safety appliances for passenger protection. The new Ripley administration, though anxious to preserve a strong liquid position, aggressively embarked on a plan to modernize its transcontinental passenger trains.

The famous *California Limited* which first began to roll between Chicago and Los Angeles on November 27, 1892, was taken out of service May 4, 1896, and did not see passengers again until late November of the same year. The new *California Limited* was a wonder of the world. An old folder states, "Our train of luxury is limited to seven through cars. It is brilliantly lighted by electricity, generated from the axles of the moving cars. It is evenly heated throughout in cool weather, and ventilated by a new process which renews the air inside several times every hour. It should also be noted that the train has a car for nearly every travel need —sightseeing, sleeping, dining, reading, writing, smoking and social gatherings." The *California Limited* became the backbone of passenger travel on the Santa Fe until advent of the modern stainless steel streamliners.

You might say it was Death Valley Scotty who blazed the trail for future Santa Fe fast trains. Scotty, who had made a fortune on the desert, chartered a Santa Fe special to whisk him from Los Angeles to Chicago in 46 hours as against the *California Limited's* running time of 66 hours. Scotty's record was unchallenged for many years.

The California Limited

Finest Train
West of Chicago

66 Hours to Los Angeles

Pullmans, Dining Car,
Buffet-Smoking Car (with Barber Shop),
Observation Car (with Ladies' Parlor),
Vestibuled and electric-lighted throughout.

Four Times a Week

Tuesdays, Wednesdays, Thursdays and Saturdays, 8:00 p.m., from Chicago, beginning November 7.

General Passenger Office,
The Atchison, Topeka & Santa Fe Railway
CHICAGO.

Santa Fe Route

The *California Limited* was reduced to four times a week during 1899. The pride of the Santa Fe resumed daily service in 1902 when the photograph below was taken. Here the *California Limited* awaits the departure hour at *La Grande* station.

The real race to the coast began with the illustrious *Deluxe*. This train carried only 60 passengers in style and comfort, plus $25 extra fare. The *Deluxe* ran once a week only, starting from Los Angeles and Chicago on Tuesday. It was plush all the way, with wicker chairs, club-baggage car with market reports, tub and shower, and even a barber. One dined in the vermillion mahogany 30-passenger diner and relaxed in the section observation. Food aboard became a conversation topic as one viewed the passing scenery or looked through the books in the library room. At night one slept in a real brass bed in a stateroom. It is said that uniformed messengers boarded the cars at San Bernardino and passed elaborate corsages to the ladies and pigskin wallets to the gentlemen.

The *Chief* became the next prestige train to ride Santa Fe rails. Service began November 14, 1926, and the first folder about the train said *extra fast, extra fine, extra fare*. It goes on to say, "As a befitting conveyance to and from the new America and the old, the Santa Fe Railway has installed the *Chief*, the most commodious and luxurious train on rails, bringing the east a business day nearer. Those who remember the Santa Fe *Deluxe* of pre-war days will appreciate the *Chief*. The *Deluxe* was the first and only extra fare train between Southern California and Chicago, and it ran but once a week. The extra fare charge was $25. The *Chief*, far more commodious and luxurious, leaves daily instead of weekly and costs less than half the old extra fare charge."

Other swift trains scorched the rails, bringing new life to California. They were the *Los Angeles Express, San Francisco Express, Overland Express, Missionary, Chicago Flyer, Navajo, Scout,* and the *Grand Canyon Limited*. The *Grand Canyon Limited* for many years was the tourist-filled vacation train which carried sleepers direct to the rim of Grand Canyon. The *Grand Canyon Limited* is the only one of the above-mentioned trains to still ply the rails from Los Angeles to Chicago.

Speed of passenger trains advanced on most runs, although the *Chief* required the same time in 1928 to reach California from Chicago as the *Deluxe* had required seventeen years earlier. In 1929, running time on most trains was cut to 58 hours each way. As passenger revenues began to drop, it was

The westbound *Los Angeles Express* hits 80 miles per hour through Rialto under a plume of black smoke. The *Los Angeles Express* ran daily Chicago to Los Angeles from 1905 until replaced by the famous *Missionary* in 1915.

obvious something had to be done. The Union Pacific in 1934 came out with a new streamliner on fast schedules behind a new motive power called the diesel. The Union Pacific planned another streamliner to be called the *City of Los Angeles*. Such a train would undermine all that the Santa Fe had left in prestige service.

As President Strong said, way back in 1874, "A railroad to be successful must also be a progressive institution. It cannot stand still if it would. If it fails to advance, it must go backward and lose ground already occupied." As if guided by these words Santa Fe secured in 1935 a two-unit diesel locomotive and conducted experimental test runs with the *Chief*. Results were impressive, and in May 1936, a new passenger train, the *Super Chief*, began to shuttle passengers between Los Angeles and Chicago. The scheduled time was 39 hours and 45 minutes, requiring an average speed of 57.3 miles per hour including stops. Chicago and California were in effect much closer together. The diesel

streamlined locomotive was complemented by a fleet of lightweight stainless steel passenger cars in 1937. The new cars were approximately half the weight of the old standard equipment, yet adequate in strength and riding quality. The appointments of the new streamliner were luxurious, although plain with pleasing colors to match the Indian design. Air conditioning was also a large selling feature and made cross country travel like an ocean breeze.

Soon to follow the streamlined *Super Chief* was the all-coach streamliner called *El Capitan*. Other name trains received the new lightweight cars except for the interruption in passenger car building caused by World War II. At war's end a steady stream of new luxuriously appointed Pullmans and chair cars flowed from the builders to join the Santa Fe fleet of famous trains.

Early in 1954, a fleet of full length dome cars brought an entirely new concept of luxury to the rail traveler. The new *Hi-Level* cars for the *El Capitan* brought new character to this all-coach train. The passenger train had come a long way from wicker chairs and brass beds.

Intra-state passenger trains were also famous in the good old days as well in modern times. Probably the most famous of the old trains were the *Saint* and the *Angel*. The *Saint* ran only to San Francisco, while the counterpart on the return to Los Angeles was the *Angel*. The two trains contained sleepers and comfortable coaches. The dining service by Fred Harvey could not be matched on any other train of its kind. Through cars on both trains operated directly to and from San Diego. The trains first saw service in 1912, but were discontinued in 1918. The Santa Fe found it hard to compete with the Southern Pacific traffic, as trains had to veer east to Barstow, thereby adding mileage and time. With the advent of a comfortable motor coach, the Santa Fe again sought a Los Angeles to San Francisco service. This move was linked with a plan to establish bus-rail-bus travel between Los Angeles, Oakland and San Francisco. The proposed scheme was to run luxury busses between Los Angeles and Bakersfield, where a connection could be made with a new streamlined all-coach train called the *Golden Gate* to Oakland, then by bus to San Francisco over the new San Francisco Bay Bridge. The new service started in 1938 and has been a success ever since.

One of the local Los Angeles to San Diego trains was also streamlined and called the *San Diegan*. This train caught on from the start and before long all local trains to San Diego were streamlined and became a part of the *San Diegan* fleet. On the way one may practically pick oranges from the train; that is, before the streamliner makes the mad dash along the shores of the Pacific before reaching San Diego.

Of all the railroad stations in California, the Santa Fe station at San Diego is among the most beautiful. This massive structure patterned along Spanish-Colonial architecture opened during the 1915 *Panama-California Exposition*. The view to the left shows the train activity during the exposition. The small switcher making up a train was former Atlantic & Pacific No. 98, built by Rome in 1889. A classic pose for a handsome 4-4-0 was in front of the San Diego station with the two big domes for a background. In the upper left, the road's most celebrated intra-state train, the *Saint*, awaits the departure hour.

The renowned *Deluxe* ran only one day a week, yet it ruled the rails on the Santa Fe between 1912 to 1917. It carried only 60 passengers, yet in a style unheard of in the annals of railroading. On the page to the left, the *Deluxe* in all its glory, atop Cajon Pass at Summit enroute to Los Angeles.

let's go

$12 round trip
To Los Angeles
───────────────── via Santa Fe

The Angel: Leaves Market Street Ferry
4:00 p. m. Daily

Superior equipment—Superior dining service
A train that is very out of the ordinary

The Saint: on the return trip offers the same
superior service.

Phone or call on me for reservations.
Jas. B. Duffy, Gen. Agt., 673 Market St., San Francisco
Phone: Kearney 315-J3371
J. J. Warner, Gen. Agt., 1218 Broadway, Oakland
Phone: Oakland 425

The only through
sleeper service between
the Exposition cities—

**very superior
service**

Phone Santa Fe city office at 334 So.
Spring St., any time day or night—
60517 — Main 738

The most famous intrastate passenger trains on the Santa Fe were *The Saint* and *The Angel*. Service began January 20, 1912, with *The Saint* running from Los Angeles to Ferry Point, connecting with the San Francisco ferry—then to Berkeley and Oakland via Richmond. The counterpart on the return to Los Angeles was called *The Angel*. The trains consist included Pullman compartment, drawing room and observation sleepers, chair car, library buffet and diner. Colorful and eye-catching advertising was issued to attract the twin city traffic. The 13-hour schedule from Los Angeles to San Francisco via Cajon Pass, Barstow and Tehachapi was rough competition to the shorter Southern Pacific route. The two trains were suspended December 31, 1918.

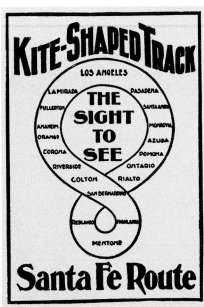

The *Kite Shaped Track* was the most beautiful short journey in Southern California. It embraced a ride over 166 miles of railway, through orange groves and scenes that appeared on the postal cards. It was unique in the fact that not one mile of the trip duplicated another. It was 1909 that the elegant new passenger station in Redlands opened its big columns to the public. (ABOVE) the *Kite Route* train pulls into Redlands on the way around the loop. Redlands development began in 1885 with the coming of the California Southern. It has always been an important citrus shipping point on the Santa Fe. San Bernardino, where the two lines of the *Kite Route* cross is shown on the right. The big wooden depot built in 1884 was destroyed by fire in 1916 and replaced by the present station. San Bernardino has always been the Santa Fe gateway to Southern California, with its shops, yards and roundhouse seething with activity.

67

Abandonment of the old California Southern mainline through Temecula Canyon left the town of Fallbrook on a branch. Heavy rains in 1916 pouring through Temecula wiped out the trackage to Oceanside. The line was rebuilt and relocated on higher ground. In the view above, the Fallbrook local at Fallbrook station. (LEFT) Under the vertical walls of Santa Margarita Canyon the local with No. 698, a 2-8-0 on the head-end chugs toward Fallbrook. While below, the local mixed pauses beside O'Neills Lake on the relocated line.

The Santa Fe has always been a pioneer in the development of motive power. Although it let the locomotive builders do the actual construction, principally the Baldwin Locomotive Works, the various experiments produced some unusual designs.

The first big contribution to motive power development came in early 1894. The Union Oil Company of California thought it had devised a system whereby a steam locomotive could use oil instead of coal for fuel. At that time Southern Pacific's coast line ran via Santa Paula and the Union Oil refinery happened to be on this mainline. Union Oil, too, was one of Southern Pacific's best freight customers. Union Oil tried to obtain the loan of a Southern Pacific steam engine for experiment and was refused, of course. Southern Pacific replied that it hauled coal from the east and from Utah at a big profit, so why should it be interested at all?

The Southern California Railway Company, a part of the Santa Fe system, was approached. The company indicated that it had no money for experiments and the engines were doing well with coal for fuel, yet an old engine would be released on loan for experiments. Locomotive No. 10 was then dispatched to Santa Paula under its own power. Mechanics went to work, trying one scheme, then another. When the final test was made, the locomotive barely managed to move. The Southern California Railway men loaded up with coal and steamed home and Southern Pacific sent Union Oil a bill for $60 for use of tracks and coal.

Undaunted, Union Oil mechanics worked on several new burners and this time collaborated with railroad shopmen at San Bernardino. Several burners were tested and eventually one with a flat nozzle that sprayed the oil over a wide area was installed forward in the firebox. The day came late in 1894 when old No. 10, powered by oil, hitched itself to a string of freight cars and headed up Cajon Pass, pulling the train without any difficulty. Thus was born the oil burning steam locomotive and immediately several others were converted to oil fuel. An ironical note, however, was the fact that the railway purchased its fuel from a competitor of Union Oil —the other company was cheaper!

The Santa Fe found an economy in oil fuel and tried to find another in the compound locomotive. Probably no other American railroad had in service as many locomotives equipped with compound cylinders as did the Santa Fe. Altogether it owned 954 compounds in wheel arrangements from 2-6-0 to 2-10-10-2. Included among them were 159 of the 2-10-2 type, which became known as the Santa Fe type locomotive.

Until the turn of the century the Santa Fe hauled most of its California tonnage with eight and ten-wheelers. Several Consolidations were used in helper service on Cajon Pass and Tehachapi grade, with the reliable 0-6-0 doing the switching.

The appearance of modern passenger types came with the advent of the Pacific type (4-6-2), first delivered to the Santa Fe in 1903. These were single

The impact of railroad station architecture on the American imagination, with its magnificent domes, windows and sweeping lines, was never better evidenced than by the *La Grande* station in Los Angeles. As Turkish as a temple in Bagdad, a nostalgic souvenir of the Golden Age of Railroading.

expansion locomotives equipped with Stephenson valve gear and numbered in the 1200 series. Pacific's delivered in the years 1905 through 1914 were of the four-cylinder balanced compound type. They were in the 1226, 1309, 1337 and 3500 classes. The Atlantic (4-4-2) passenger locomotive also made its appearance on the Santa Fe during 1903 as a balanced compound type.

Several mallets were tried on Cajon Pass at various times. From the Baldwin Locomotive Works in 1909 came two 4-4-6-2 and two 2-8-8-2 type locomotives. The 4-4-6-2 type were assigned to road passenger service and the 2-8-8-2 type as helpers. Ten articulated compounds of the 2-10-10-2 type were built at the Topeka shops from 2-10-2 locomotives of the 900 and 1600 classes for the high-pressure units and the low-pressure units were purchased new from the Baldwin Locomotive Works. In 1911 these were transferred to California for helper service on Cajon Pass and at the time were the most powerful locomotives in the world. The usual make-up of a hill train placed the road engine on the point, then the mallet some 29 cars back. If

more power was needed, additional helpers were placed just ahead of the caboose.

Frank McNeil, an oldtime Santa Fe engineer, tells of the time when he had one of the 2-10-10-2 mallets on Cajon Pass. He was on a drag freight with No. 3003 and started down grade after passing Summit. As he began to roll with the freight headed for San Bernardino he lost control of the air. He said, "The only reason I am alive today is that blasted train could not shove them mallets faster than 30 miles per hour on any grade."

To show a sampling of Santa Fe's thinking along motive power lines the Baldwin Locomotive Works was requested in 1915 to draw up plans for the greatest mallet of all time. It was to be a quadruplex double compound of the 2-8-8-8-8-2 wheel arrangement. Two cabs were included, one in the front and one in the usual position over the firebox. Needless to say, this hypothetical giant never left the drawing boards. From then on Santa Fe stuck pretty close to non-articulated steam motive power.

The first Mountain type (4-8-2) passenger locomotives of the 3700 class were given trials in 1918.

OVERLEAF

The huge, low-pressure front cylinders which are the hallmark of a true mallet are abundantly visible as a 2-10-10-2 thunders around a high fill on Cajon Pass just west of Victorville.

"Largest and most powerful passenger locomotives in existence", was the term Baldwin used in 1909 when they delivered two 4-4-6-2 compound mallets to Santa Fe. Complete with 73-inch drivers, low pressure cylinders, and passenger type tenders, the mallets were fast. Built with road numbers 1300-01, they were renumbered 1398-99, when the view on the left was made as the big mallet pulled into San Bernardino. No. 3000, first of ten 2-10-10-2 compounds is shown above. Two of the big giants shown below await helper assignments at San Bernardino in 1916.

BOTH TRAINS MAGAZINE COLLECTION

71

HARLAN
HINEY
1963

California is reached in the most comfortable manner over the Santa Fé Route—Atchison, Topeka, & Santa Fé R. R.—through sleeping-cars run from both Chicago and St. Louis without change.

They were so popular from the start that Santa Fe secured a total of 51 by 1924. These locomotives were used on most of the passenger runs along with the new Pacific type (4-6-2) of the 3400 class. The big Northern type (4-8-4) locomotives began to arrive in 1927. These massive locomotives with 73-inch and 80-inch drivers appeared in four classes. The 3751 class in 1927, the 3765 class in 1937, and the 3776 class in 1941, with the last group arriving in the war years as the 2900 class.

The first diesel was a 600 horsepower Alco switcher which began shoving cars in the Chicago yards in 1935. Hard on the heels of the switcher was the first diesel passenger locomotive, consisting of two 1,800 horsepower units. This streamlined locomotive was carefully road tested on the *Chief* and later assigned to the new train called the *Super Chief*. A number of passenger diesels followed in rapid succession. By 1940, the diesel invasion was on in earnest. It was that year when the Santa Fe road-tested the first diesel freight locomotive to be built for American service. Tests were conclusive in favor of the diesel. The influence of these pioneer tests conducted on the Santa Fe paved the way for rapid change over of the system. These tests demonstrated many economies in operation, but the big item was water, an item needed in huge quantities by steam locomotives. Previously, water for steam locomotives had to be hauled in by tank car at considerable expense. This saving alone made the diesel look good to top management and operating officials.

The role of the Santa Fe in carrying tremendous volumes of traffic to California during World War II is a point to be well remembered. During the spring of 1943 the Santa Fe rails handled five times more westbound traffic than it handled in 1938. By 1945, it was doubled to ten times the 1938 peak volume. Without modern steam power and a large stable of diesel locomotives, the Santa Fe would have folded under the strain. To bolster the war

effort, thirty 4-8-4 steam locomotives of the 2900 class were added to the roster. These giants complete with 80-inch drivers and roller bearings handled some of the longest steam locomotive runs known to railroading.

In the years following World War II, successive purchases of more diesels meant eventual death for the iron horse. At one time, fifteen steam locomotives were required to handle a single passenger train between Los Angeles and Chicago. One diesel locomotive could take the entire train all the way with only change of crews. The water problem brought about complete dieselization during 1954.

Although the steam locomotive is gone from the rails of the Santa Fe, we can still miss it. To many it was more than a machine; it was a personality. It was almost as though, in the process of its creation, the steam locomotive absorbed certain qualities and characteristics of those mortals who built it. If the heritage of the Santa Fe must be reduced to a phrase, it should be that the nation's greatest railroad will not in 1963, or in any year, forsake its steam heritage.

Under President Fred Gurley, the Santa Fe became known as "America's New Railroad." New cars, new locomotives, new yards, new tracks, new communication methods, new streamliners and new freight service. During 1954, a whole new streamliner, the *San Francisco Chief*, began to roll from Chicago to San Francisco in 47½ hours.

The Santa Fe continues to progress with Ernest S. Marsh at the throttle. The new president instituted new *Hi-Level* passenger equipment for the *El Capitan*, new freight services and improvements all along the line. So it goes day-after-day on the Santa Fe—this building of "America's New Railroad." For only by constantly building and rebuilding can a railroad stay new and ready for the future.

Old Colonel Holliday was decidedly headed in the right direction.

HERE THE WEST BEGINS . . . at the bumper post of the Los Angeles Union Passenger Terminal, where drumhead signatures of Santa Fe streamliners glow in the dusk. The magnificent terminal is a beautiful architectural appreciation to the early Spanish culture of old California. The terminal is not imposing in height—the square clock tower rising only 125 feet surrounded by the station, its buildings, tracks and ramps covering 48 acres. When the terminal opened in May 1939, the swarming hordes of Los Angeles citizenry came to the celebration and climbed all over Santa Fe's rolling exhibit shown on the right. (CENTER) In the hushed quiet of the long waiting room the traveler sinks down into a leather settee. (BELOW) Nearly 500 feet of gleaming subway concourse connect the station proper with eight loading platforms serving 16 sets of tracks.

A switcher moves a cut of mail cars beside the postal terminal annex. (UPPER-RIGHT) The pre-war *California Limited* awaits the departure hour in the stub-end terminal. (LOWER-RIGHT) Along the well manicured right-of-way of Los Angeles Union Passenger Terminal the wartime *San Diegan* rounds a curve and heads into the sun. (BELOW) A symphony of escaping steam joins the trainmen as they gather under the trainshed.

BOTH DONALD DUKE

SANTA FE RAILWAY—DON ERB

STAN KISTLER

Mission Tower, a quarter mile outside the main terminal, is the control point for dispatching trains to their proper carriers. The San Bernardino local shown above passes the tower on the run to Pasadena. (CENTER) Motor car local crosses the Southern Pacific iron and heads into the terminal. (BELOW) The towerman at the terminal throat is surrounded by the tools of his calling. (OPPOSITE PAGE) The famous Hi-Level *El Capitan* prepares for departure under the lights of winter. (BELOW) The *El Capitan* departs LAUPT in the glow of a long summer evening.

DONALD DUKE

THE Chief SantaFe

In 1926, the Deluxe was succeeded by the *Chief*, daily all-Pullman luxury train. Complete with barber and bath, valet and maid, soda fountain and cigar stand, and luxurious cuisine catered by Fred Harvey. The *Chief* became the "number one" train on the Santa Fe. In its sedate diners ate the biggest names on the flickering screen. The *Chief* established a reputation as the conveyance of the elite from coast to coast. The monarch of the rails was known as extra fine, extra fast, and $10 extra fare. Plans to streamline the *Chief* were announced in 1937, with a new 50¾ hour schedule. On February 22, 1938, the *Chief* went stainless steel with 10 streamline cars consisting of a mail car, baggage-mail, club-baggage, club-lounge, five sleepers and a sleeper observation. The big red and silver diesel did not appear until late 1946. The *Chief* had its origins in the era of standard Pullmans and has survived the streamlining age with a reputation of fine appointments almost undimmed by time. The time-honored *Chief* still makes its daily run on a 39¾ hour schedule. (ABOVE) The sound and fury of big locomotives ascending Cajon Pass can be heard from the heavyweight Pullman cars of the great *Chief* way back in 1933. (LOWER-RIGHT) Amidst the wild and gloomy rock formations of the San Gabriel Mountains, the *Chief* in steam and stainless steel climbs the west approach of Cajon Pass. (ABOVE-RIGHT) The observation car at the rear of the standard *Chief* offered an atmosphere of spacious luxury.

The *Chief* bridged the transitional gap between the age of Pullman standards and the steam locomotive, the diesel era and streamlining. (ABOVE) The semi-streamlined *Chief* rolls up the eastside of Cajon Pass under a cloud of black smoke. (LEFT) The tail end in oval symmetry completes the full dressed *Chief*. (UPPER-RIGHT) The *Chief* streamliner with full length dome lounge passes through the high desert near Victorville. (LOWER-RIGHT) The Santa Fe converted 11 freight diesel sets of 4-units each to passenger service in 1946-48. Here the *Chief* near Pine Lodge hummed behind one of the converted units.

The blunt nose of Santa Fe's first passenger diesel signaled the coming of a famous fleet of streamliners. On May 12, 1936, the Santa Fe placed on a once a week schedule of 39¾ hours, the *Super Chief*, a train of standard Pullman equipment drawn by a 3,600 horsepower multiple-unit locomotive. Painted black, cobalt, saratoga blue, golden olive and pimpernel scarlet, each unit carried the Santa Fe emblem and a streaming headdress of an Indian Chief and the name *Super Chief* etched in heavy glass panels set into each end. (BELOW) In all its glory, the first westbound run arrives at Pasadena station with a throng of spectators on hand to view the new monarch of the rails. (RIGHT) Several nights later, the first eastbound run rolls into Pasadena under a blaze of lights and a repeat performance. The heavyweight train was withdrawn on May 18, 1937, when nine lightweight stainless steel cars built by Budd were placed in service. The new *Super Chief* was really super with super luxury, super comfort and super time between Los Angeles and Chicago. This streamline train consisted of five Pullmans, diner, lounge, mail and baggage car. Each car was named after an Indian pueblo and the decorative schemes of the car interiors were a blend of Navajo Indian motif. A second streamliner built by Pullman-Standard arrived February 22, 1938, thus the once a week schedule was increased to twice a week from 1938 to 1946. After the war, when new equipment became available, a daily schedule was planned and took effect February 29, 1948. Only three years later in 1951, a new world standard for rail travel was set. The entire *Super Chief* was re-equipped with ultra-modern sleepers, diner and dome-lounge featuring the Turquoise Room. The *Super Chief* is still "number one" on the Santa Fe's passenger roster.

ALLAN YOUELL

G. M. BEST

STAN KISTLER

Everything is super about the *Super Chief*, with super cuisine, super crew and super service. (RIGHT) The *Super Chief* pulls into Pasadena in the morning behind the roads only Fairbanks-Morse passenger diesel locomotives. (UPPER-LEFT) The *Super Chief* as it appeared in 1937 with the streamline consist. (LOWER-LEFT) The westbound *Super Chief* invades Pasadena in 1946 with diesel No. 15.

STAN KISTLER

A new world standard for the transcontinental coach traveler was set by the Santa Fe when, on February 22, 1938, two all-coach trains began to glide smoothly between Los Angeles and Chicago. Called *El Capitan*, the sleek diesel powered seven car silver train first operated twice a week; every-other-day in 1946; and daily in 1948 on a fast 39¾ hour schedule. In the year 1956, when the trend was toward low slung trains, the Santa Fe introduced the new $13 million "Hi-Level" Floating comfort eight feet above the rail, the new cars seated 78 in luxury coach seats with washroom, baggage and vestibule on the lower level. The lounge is located on both levels and food for the 86-seat diner is transported on an elevator from the kitchen below. Today, *El Capitan* is still captain of the all-coach streamliners. (ABOVE) *El Capitan*, a complete caravan for the cross country coach traveler, wheels its way through the Southern California town of Upland with the pre-war consist and diesel whose speed needle touches the 80 miles per hour mark.

The gingerbread covered station of South Pasadena watched a different world roll by its door daily in the form of the sleek all-coach streamliner *El Capitan*. The old station was sentenced to oblivion in 1941, but saved when the second World War came and restricted new materials. The old faithful finally fell to the wrecker in 1954. (TOP) The one step vestibule of the "Hi-Level". (ABOVE) The "Hi-Level" *El Capitan* climbs the grade of Cajon Pass in a clear Southern California afternoon.

The two-car diner, club-lounge and soda fountain was at the head end of the train. This saved the passengers from passing through the car to reach the other end of the train. (LEFT) Daytime travel in the luxury of green plush, inlaid wood and electric lamps that glimmered with polished brass.

Luxury travel to California in 1903 meant the *California Limited* which made the run from Chicago to Los Angeles in 68 hours. The service was exceptional, the accommodations superb and the cuisine by Fred Harvey luxurious. By 1910, the *California Limited* was re-equipped from locomotive to observation car, with deep recessed platform, vapor steam heating and guaranteed dust free. The new cars were built by Pullman, a certificate of quality to the experienced traveler. At Summit, atop Cajon Pass, uniformed boys boarded the Pullmans with free boutonnieres for the gentlemen and roses for the ladies. The *California Limited* was Santa Fe's first name train when it began to roll on November 27, 1892. It operated almost continuously until the middle 1950's. (ABOVE) Seven sections of the *California Limited* were common. At one time the train was dispatched in 23 sections westbound and 22 sections eastbound in the same day. (BELOW) The wistful loneliness of the California desert with miles of mesquite, sagebrush and Joshua trees presents a dramatic panorama as the Pullman section of the *California Limited* lifts itself up Cajon Pass, its smoke blowing to far horizons.

DONALD DUKE

97

The *California Limited* behind a double-header climbs the serpentine tracks raising it from the high desert to the summit of Cajon Pass. (BELOW) A mighty 4-8-4 coils the *California Limited* around an elevated curve over-crossing the east-bound mainline near Victorville.

The 13-car *Golden Gate* streamliner of today thunders out of Bakersfield under the protection of modern Centralized Traffic Control. The three-unit General Motors diesel locomotive heads the train across the rich San Joaquin Valley with Richmond as the final destination.

SANTA FE RAILWAY

1938 was a Santa Fe year. On July 1, the Santa Fe inaugurated an unusual rail-bus project in connection with the superb streamliner named the *Golden Gate.* In the service, passengers were handled between the new downtown station in San Francisco and the San Pablo station in Oakland by means of modern buses operating over the new San Francisco-Oakland Bay Bridge. Between Oakland and Bakersfield, two *Golden Gate* trains each made one round trip on a fast schedule. At Bakersfield, passengers were taken by buses to Los Angeles. The identical trains each consisted of stainless steel cars air-conditioned throughout and drawn by 1,800 horsepower diesels. Each train carried a baggage car, three beautiful coaches, a Fred Harvey lunch counter-diner, and a parlor observation car. Today the coordination of these modern facilities continues to link Los Angeles with San Francisco on fast schedules. (ABOVE) A modern parlor observation car at Bakersfield wearing the *Golden Gate* emblem. (UPPER-RIGHT) Convenient routes to Los Angeles via Hollywood, Glendale or Pasadena make the co-ordinated run convenient to the traveling public. (FAR-RIGHT) The *Golden Gate* heads into the afternoon sun as it approaches Richmond. On the right, diesel motor No. 9 rolls the seven-car *Golden Gate* through El Cerrito between Berkeley and Richmond. Motor No. 9 handled the first northbound schedule from Bakersfield to Oakland.

STAN KISTLER

The Valley Flyer, a six-car steam passenger train was placed in service June 11, 1939, between Bakersfield and Oakland to connect at both cities with modern buses for San Francisco and Los Angeles. *The Valley Flyer* was to supplement the popular diesel-powered *Golden Gate* operating between the same points. The new air-conditioned train was made up of rebuilt standard cars and was a study in modernistic design and bright coloring. The train consist comprised one combination baggage-club car, one refreshment car, three coaches and a diner. The train left Bakersfield daily at 6:30 am and arrived in Oakland at 12:35 pm. The return run left Oakland at 1:55 pm which arrived in Bakersfield at 8:00 pm. (ABOVE) The bright red, yellow and silver *Valley Flyer* pulls into Oakland on the first day of operation. (LEFT) Front end of the train. This was Santa Fe's first attempt at streamlining older steam power. (UPPER-RIGHT) The afternoon train departed Oakland and headed up the middle of the street before reaching the open right-of-way north of Berkeley. (LOWER-RIGHT) Rolling through the countryside east of Luzon.

The *San Francisco Chief* was inaugurated on a daily schedule June 6, 1954. High point of the new deluxe equipment was the all-dome lounge car. This new train filled a definite need for luxury travel between the San Joaquin Valley and the Southwest. The *Chief* made the run to Chicago on a fast schedule of 47½ hours operating by way of the Texas panhandle and Oklahoma. It replaced the San Francisco section of the *Grand Canyon Limited*. On the left, modern buses greet the passengers at Richmond for the continued trip to Berkeley, Oakland and San Francisco. (BELOW) Beautiful fields of orange and yellow California poppies add color to the *San Francisco Chief* as it rolls toward Richmond. (UPPER-RIGHT) The *Chief* stretched around the Tehachapi Loop beside a mile long freight on the siding. In the upper right, the *Chief* crosses Muir trestle near Glen Frazer.

STAN KISTLER   SANTA FE RAILWAY

SANTA FE RAILWAY—R. COLLINS BRADLEY

Throughout the closing decades of steam, the ruling power of the San Joaquin Valley was the Pacific type locomotive. Caught on the westbound *Grand Canyon Limited,* No. 3445 highballs out of Bakersfield under a cloud of smoke.

Santa Fe's M-131, diesel motor car, rumbles across the Kings River bridge near Dinuba on the Fresno-Corcoran run via Visalia. (CENTER) The *Grand Canyon Limited*, soon to be replaced by the *San Francisco Chief*, prepares to leave Oakland station in 1952. The *Golden Gate* on the right still holds the blue flag. (LOWER) During the second World War, the *Golden Gate* rolls behind a trim Atlantic type with big 79-inch driver's massively forcing flanged wheel against steel rail. The Atlantics often were called upon to substitute for the *Golden Gate's* overworked diesels.

The tourist-filled *Grand Canyon Limited* is one of America's most popular vacation trains. It began June 9, 1929, as an economy train and has operated daily ever since. At Williams, sleepers are cut off and run direct to the South Rim of Grand Canyon. The running time of 58 hours Chicago to Los Angeles was cut June 8, 1947, to 48 hours 45 minutes, and streamline cars have been added to the consist. The train usually operated in three sections; one Chicago to Los Angeles via Raton Pass; one Chicago to San Francisco via Texas panhandle (discontinued after introduction of *San Francisco Chief*); one Chicago to Los Angeles via Texas panhandle. On the right, the eastbound *Grand Canyon Limited* runs around a freight on Cajon. (BELOW) With a clear track, the *Grand Canyon Limited* steams toward Arizona.

The friendly conductor going about his duties. (BELOW) Throughout the closing decades of steam, the ruling power on the *Grand Canyon Limited* was the 2900 class 4-8-4, shown climbing the westside of Cajon Pass.

The mailing and receiving of letters, parcel post and express has become so much a part of everyday American life that few give a thought to the vital part the Santa Fe plays in speeding the mail to your door. The most famous and fastest of the great mail trains is the *Fast Mail and Express*, trains Nos. 7-8. These trains operate daily between Chicago and Los Angeles-San Francisco on passenger train schedules and during rush periods operate in many sections. Before the second World War, Nos. 7-8 were scheduled in the public timetable with notation that the train would carry a limited number of coach passengers in the combination car used for the crew riders on the rear end. On the right, the mail pouch is caught on the fly at a small way station and then sorted down enroute as shown below. On the left, the *Fast Mail and Express* climbs Cajon Pass in the days of steam.

The smart all-coach streamliner *San Diegan* caught the
popular fancy from the start. The shimmering six-car,
stainless steel train was first put in operation March 27,
1938. The new train made two round trips daily on a 2½
hour schedule between Los Angeles and San Diego with
just a single set of equipment. The train consisted of
diesel locomotive No. 7, a baggage-mail car, four coaches,
a cheery tavern-lunch counter diner and a parlor observation car. A second train was added during 1940, thus providing four streamline *San Diegan* trains in each direction.
Approximately the same schedule exists today, however
additional coaches are added to handle the increased
patronage. For many miles, the Santa Fe tracks unwind
along the coastal strip and cling to the bluffs overlooking
the sea. (ABOVE) Between the cliffs and the pounding
surf, the *San Diegan* rolls along the sandy beach of San
Clemente. On the left, the *San Diegan* prepares to cross
the Whittier line of the Pacific Electric at Los Nietos Junction. Due to increased patronage, this short train replaced
the two-car RDC units.

RICHARD STEINHEIMER

One of the most revolutionary trends in modern railroading has been the introduction of streamlined, lightweight, stainless steel passenger equipment. From the beginning, the new *San Diegan* was an institution and grew from one train to a fleet in a short period of time. (ABOVE) In its youth, the last scheduled *San Diegan* for the night pulls into San Diego behind motor No. 7 and ties up. (UPPER-RIGHT) City officials and the citizenry of San Diego were on hand March 27, 1938 to welcome the first run of the *San Diegan* streamliner. (LOWER-RIGHT) During August 1947, the 13-car *San Diegan* rolls down Linda Vista grade behind motor No. 8 and No. 5. In a short 20 minutes the sleek silver streamliner will pull in front of the San Diego station. The first revenue car is a through Pullman from the *Chief*, however this service lasted only a short time.

DONALD DUKE

RDC means rail diesel car. The Santa Fe operated two RDC's between Los Angeles and San Diego as a single multiple-unit train. The maiden day for the RDC service in Southern California was May 21, 1952. On two runs, non-stop service was provided on the 128 mile run on a schedule of 2 hours and 15 minutes—30 minutes faster than previous schedules. Along with the *San Diegan* streamliners and the local, the RDC's gave seven regular schedules each way daily. Due to the limited seating capacity, the RDC's were replaced by a full *San Diegan* streamliner. (ABOVE) Rolling along the shoreline of the blue Pacific, the RDC's clip along through San Clemente at 75 miles per hour. (RIGHT) The brakeman sets up the marker lamps. On the left, the non-stop *San Diegan* accelerates through Rivera on the way to Los Angeles.

STAN KISTLER

TRAIN TIME TABLE PACIFIC STANDARD TIME			
NO	NORTHBOUND	NO	SOUTHBOUND
71	R 5:42 AM	70	F 3:14 AM
73	F 7:27 AM	78	F 6:54 PM
75	R 12:29 PM		
77	R 4:54 PM		

71 RUNS DAILY EXCEPT SUN & HOLI'S
R FLAG STOP TO RECEIVE PASSGS FOR LA
F DENOTES FLAG STOP
USE WHITE FLAG TO STOP TRAINS

Mrs. J. B. MacDonald of Encinitas makes a trip to Los Angeles twice a month to visit her daughter. The small seaside town is not a regular stop on the San Diego line, but Mrs. MacDonald is an expert at flagging the *San Diegan* that normally whips through town at 80 miles per hour. Mrs. MacDonald said, "When I see her coming around the bend down there, I grab that white flag and get right out in the middle of the track and wave the flag like HELL till the engineer blasts me off with his horn. I've almost been run over a couple of times before they could get the train stopped." (LOWER) With smoke trailing its path, the Los Angeles bound local charges through Pacific Beach behind a Baldwin built 4-6-2.

STAN KISTLER

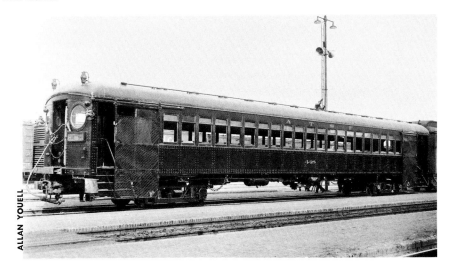

ALLAN YOUELL

The white surf rolls gently up the beach at high tide as the present day *San Diegan* rolls along the Pacific at San Clemente. The Alco units with their large and squarish noses accented neatly by a grilled headlight casing present a welcome change from EMD's bulldog front end. (LEFT) Troop movements between Los Angeles and San Diego during World War II used former Southern Pacific-Red Electric interurban cars. The non-electric trailers had big gates at the ends, spoked wheels and rattan seats with three on one side and two on the other. Trains were made up of 10 to 12 cars with standard couplers on each end of the set. Service speed was restricted to 50 miles per hour on these classic trains. The original owner was the U.S. Maritime Commission, however the cars were later lettered ATSF.

R. P. MIDDLEBROOK

The semi-streamlined equipment of the former *Valley Flyer* found a new home on the San Diego line during the early 1940's. The air-conditioned consist featured a club-baggage, coaches and a diner all decked out in silver and red and yellow stripes. (BELOW) The steam powered *San Diegan* crosses onto the double track as it nears Hobart Tower south of Los Angeles. (LEFT) The high cliffs along the oceans edge prevented a sea-level entry into San Diego via the famed La Jolla beach resort. Thus the only way around was up and over the foothills with Linda Vista as the summit. Here the standard green pre-war coach train behind two engines climbs toward San Diego. (LOWER-LEFT) With 13 cars of turf enthusiasts, the *Del Mar Special* thunders along the Pacific north of Oceanside.

122

After World War I, traffic declines on railroad branch lines brought about by highway competition created interest in the self-propelled rail motor car. The development of the gasoline engine and mechanical transmission designed for motor trucks was responsible for the introduction of the rail motor car for local and branch line service. The Santa Fe purchased many of these cars and even during the 1950's, the M-181 ran daily between Los Angeles and San Bernardino. On the right, the local pulls into Pasadena. (BELOW) She rumbles across the Arroyo Seco trestle, while the view in the upper left shows the M-181 passing the Arcadia Tower, crossing the Pacific Electric, route of the *Big Red Cars* to Monrovia and Glendora. (LOWER-LEFT) At Fresno, the Fresno-Corcoran motor local loads the mail for the days run to Visalia.

STAN KISTLER

Through the wildly desolate beauty of Cajon Pass, the Santa Fe climbs out of the coastal valley at San Bernardino and into the Mojave desert north of the San Gabriel Mountains. The route shared with the Union Pacific includes two single-track lines built at different times on different grades, but used as double track. Cajon Pass is unique in that it is not a pass through a mountain, but between mountain ranges. To the east is the San Bernardino range; to the west the San Gabriels. Cajon in Spanish means box or geographically a box-like canyon. Helpers were an institution on Cajon. They were inevitably slow, ponderous beasts of high tractive effort, but beautiful to watch like the 2-10-2's shown in the accompanying photographs. (RIGHT) Under rolling clouds of oil smoke and 86 cars on the drawbar, a brace of powerful 2-10-2's shove an eastbound extra through tunnel No. 2 at Alray. While above, more ancient yet symmetrical 2-10-2's assist extra 3855 East above Cajon station. Cut in the middle of a freight consist, No. 3850 on the left, does her part working the grade near Summit.

124

The sunset of steam lay over the land when these illustrations were made in the glorious setting of Cajon Pass. On the right, with throttles wide open and reverse gears locked in the notch, a 2-8-2 with a husky 4-8-4 send steam and smoke skyward as they work eastbound tonnage up the westside. (ABOVE) A long freight with two at the rear make a dramatic sequence of motive power in tandem. On the desert side shown below, No. 3935 and No. 3897 work a westbound manifest up Cajon.

BOTH STAN KISTLER

There is something singular about the telegraph office, something that gives it a distinction that nothing else in railroading possesses. It stands, day and night, guarding the ebb and flow of traffic, unperturbed as the *Super Chief* descends on it and shakes the foundations. Such an office is at Summit, where Santa Fe and Union Pacific trains trudge up the slopes of Cajon Pass, perhaps pause to pick up orders or cut off a helper or two, then slip away down the mountain, their course traced across the distances by brief notations on the wire.

DONALD DUKE

Dramatic and unaccustomed is the teaming of this graceful, high-wheeled Pacific steam locomotive with a powerful 4-8-4 on the drawbar heading east on the long grade west of Summit. On the right, in the year it was dieselized, the *Chief* carried at its rear a belated tribute to the great carbuilder in the form of an enclosed observation-lounge car *George M. Pullman,* shown gliding through Summit beside Union Pacific and Santa Fe helpers.

The unceasing parade of steam power over Cajon Pass in the great days reached all-time high during the second World War, when the smoke from five freights climbing out of San Bernardino could be seen. (RIGHT) Against a snow-mantled backdrop, the eastbound *El Tovar* grips the rails near Gish. (CENTER-RIGHT) No. 1621 handles the smoky end of a 60-car freight at Alray. (LOWER-RIGHT) A brace of growling diesels pilot a thundering 2-10-2 and her charge west of Victorville. Immemorial pungency of oil smoke, hot metal and diesel oil fill the desert air below, while a 2-8-2 pulls the slack from a drag freight and charges up the eastside of Cajon.

131

Silver rails and stainless steel manifest the desert in constant changes of tones and colors as night appears. (RIGHT) Over the desert, its smoke trailing to far California horizons, a section of the celebrated *Navajo* charges the grade west of Victorville behind a mighty 3751 class 4-8-4, in the days when the diesel was unheard of and steam ruled the high iron from Chicago to the Pacific. (ABOVE-RIGHT) The towering San Gabriel Mountains background the eastbound tourist filled *Grand Canyon Limited* as she rounds the bend at Alray.

In 1951, steam ruled the *Grand Canyon Limited*, crack tourist train of the Santa Fe. Here on the left, in a camera portrait, the enormous 4-8-4 built during the second World War, with 18 cars bound for Los Angeles is getting underway west of Victorville. The dark clouds of rain gather in the West, the rear brakeman on the right, mounts the caboose platform, lights a fusee and prepares to head back up the track to protect the rear of his train. (BELOW) A dramatic panorama of sleek stainless steel and streamlined diesel, still requiring the helper horsepower of one of the road's celebrated 4-8-4 type to command the grade of Cajon Pass.

SANTA FE RAILWAY—R. COLLINS BRADLEY

BOTH STAN KISTLER

Oddity of the desert is the gaunt, grotesque Joshua Tree, a species of desert foliage found abundantly on California's Mojave Desert. Here a desert monarch stands in a vast region of stark desolation casting shadows on the passing rhythm of crossheads and reciprocating siderods of a passing train.

The rhythm of crossheads and reciprocating siderods dim the growl of a Union Pacific stock extra as No. 3866, a Santa Fe type 2-10-2 charges across the tracks in the San Bernardino yards. The Union Pacific diesel train will follow the steamer down the shared AT&SF Third District tracks to Riverside Junction. Here the UP freight will take off on its own rails to Los Angeles and the Santa Fe will head for Los Angeles via Fullerton. (LEFT) In Cajon Pass, eastbound between Alray and Summit, No. 3850 struggles upgrade with 87 cars on its straining drawbar while working its way toward Barstow. With flanges squealing and wooden stock cars rocking at every curve, the mighty 2-10-2 shatters the windswept solitude.

The name San Bernardino was given to a settlement by a party of missionaries from the San Gabriel Mission who entered the valley on May 20, 1810, the feast day of San Bernardino de Siena. In 1851, Captain Jefferson Hunt arrived in the region with a party of 500 Mormons from Salt Lake and established the town of San Bernardino. The region as an industrial and railroad center began in 1887 when the Santa Fe consolidated its shops next to the town. Locomotive erecting shops, machine shops and car shops for the coast lines were built, along with the division headquarters with large yards and roundhouse. Today very little has changed except the erecting shops do heavy repairs on diesel power instead of steam. (ABOVE) Train time at San Bernardino depot with the *Chief* on the left, the *Grand Canyon Limited* taking the center, and a hefty 2-10-2 on the right resigned to yard goat service. (UPPER-RIGHT) Aerial view of the giant roundhouse, shops, yards and depot. (LOWER-RIGHT) The roar of the overhead crane fills the air while the ground vibrates to the rhythm of air hammers at the erecting shop.

Santa Fe No. 3891, a ponderous 2-10-2 rolls off the turnable at San Bernardino, preparatory to helping shove a tonnage train up the westside of Cajon Pass. (BELOW) A yard goat gathers a freight together in the large San Bernardino yards. The shops are visible to the left of the engine. (UPPER-LEFT) The engine hostler eases out on the throttle and the big engine clatters across the turntable. Note the speed recorder box at the left of the throttle. (LOWER-LEFT) The San Bernardino roundhouse, the garage for steam locomotives, was mirky and full of strange noises. Usually a dozen engines were in, some of them just off the road and belching plumes of black smoke into the flues over their stacks. Others puffing a not so black breath as they got up steam for the long climb up Cajon Pass.

Stretches of desolate sand dunes, dry lakes and distant buttes shimmering in the heat — this is the great American desert. After crossing the heaped masses of Cajon Pass, the Santa Fe rails traverse this dry, arid expanse of desert with unevenly sloping valleys and canyons. Only the cottonwood on the banks of the mighty Colorado relieve the tedium of the rolling sagebrush landscape. Ludlow, midway between Barstow and Needles, once was a junction with the desert railroads and outpost for Death Valley. Here in the frontier days of gold, silver and borate, trains of the Ludlow & Southern and Tonopah & Tidewater met the mainline of the Santa Fe. The shops of the Tonopah & Tidewater were located at Ludlow and formed a panorama against the desert waste. The engine house in the center of the view below, shows a line of five engines from the famed Bullfrog & Goldfield and Borate & Daggett railroads. Note the interesting balloon track used to turn passenger trains around in the good old days. On the far right track, a small Ludlow & Southern train waits patiently before heading east, then south for Stedman.

It takes a lot of things to run a locomotive, but the most important item on the desert is water. Here, next to the Tonopah & Tidewater yard, No. 1300 takes a long drink at Ludlow before taking on the long stretch of track to Needles. (BELOW) Thundering up the slight grade out of Ludlow, a long freight under a cloud of smoke heads west toward Barstow. The Tonopah & Tidewater private car *Boron* stands under its canopy in the blistering sun.

Reaching the towering Tehachapi Mountains, the Southern Pacific tracks during 1874 came to an abrupt halt. Here the engineers faced the problem of raising the railroad tracks 2,734 feet from the San Joaquin Valley floor at Caliente to the top of the mountain pass, an elevation of 4,025 feet in 16 miles as the crow flies. This feat was accomplished by swerving 28 miles of tracks in serpentine fashion around gradual curves on a 2.2 per cent grade through 18 tunnels. At one point, the track looped over itself in a remarkable stroke of engineering. The Loop has since become one of the seven wonders of the railroading world. The Santa Fe obtained trackage rights over the 67.38 miles of railroad from Mojave to Kern Junction (Bakersfield) as part of the purchase of the Mojave-Needles line way back in 1899. Like a giant sentry, the semaphore on the left, guards the east portal of the Loop tunnel as an immense 2-10-2 holes through the bore and curves around the lofty circle forming the Loop. High above on a siding, a double-headed freight prepares to roll downgrade and through the same tunnel on its way to Bakersfield. The Santa Fe stuck with the 2-10-2 for tonnage on the same grades which rival Southern Pacific ran cab-in-front articulateds. (ABOVE) During the Korean conflict, a train of deadhead troop Pullmans leans into the curve of the Loop, doubleheaded with a 4-8-2 and 4-8-4.

The great Tehachapi Loop on the left, is located high on the mountain where the shining thread of railroad tracks swing in a huge circle, rapidly descending from the top, it disappears into the mouth of a tunnel. A complete circle, 3,795 feet in circumference has been completed. (BELOW) A dramatic panorama of the Tehachapi Loop in its celebrated form with a Santa Fe freight, powered by four engines cut into the consist at intervals, passes over itself as it emerges from the tunnel that is one of the Loop's interesting features. Note the Southern Pacific freight at the extreme left, also another freight coming up the grade at the extreme right of the view. (UPPER-RIGHT) A long freight stretched around the famous Loop. In the center, the *Scout* curves into the Loop enroute to Barstow and the East.

Nothing in the glory days of steam railroading so excited the beholder as a double-header, a train so gigantic or so heavy as to require two locomotives. (ABOVE) A double-header has just conquered Tehachapi and rolls downgrade near Walong with the *Scout*. On the left, the San Francisco connection of the *Grand Canyon Limited* climbs Tehachapi, rounds the Loop, then heads for Barstow. (UPPER-RIGHT) Against a backdrop of the imposing Tehachapi Mountains, the *Scout* drifts down through Woodford, ahead is the vast plain of the San Joaquin Valley. (LOWER-RIGHT) A 60-car train of brilliant yellow and orange refrigerator cars winds its way up the mountain grade of Tehachapi from Mojave hauled by a powerful Santa Fe type steamer.

Framed through a gnarled oak tree, the blue and yellow freight diesel shown above, snakes its way up the westside of Tehachapi Pass. Rounding the Caliente horseshoe grade, Extra No. 3721 digs in for the long climb up the mountain from the valley below. (RIGHT) No. 3840 in mid-train gives an extra push to a long drag of swaying freight cars as they twist and turn around Caliente loop before reaching the heavy grade of the pass. Only minutes before, this same train passed the water tank in the upper right. Here is where eastbound trains go west, and westbound trains go east! (UPPER-RIGHT) The diesel hidden by the venerable 4-8-2 works its way around the serpentine tracks of Tehachapi grade with the *Grand Canyon Limited.*

153

With a clear track ahead all the way to Richmond, a valley freight behind double-headed power slowly gathers itself together with two 4-6-2's doing the honors in the great tradition of steam railroading. (UPPER-RIGHT) Two high stepping Pacific type locomotives emerge from the Glen Frazer bore under a cloud of hot steam. (LOWER-RIGHT) A vintage side door caboose skips along as No. 1971, a Consolidation pulling 27 cars blasts the summer afternoon with exhaust from the stack.

W. C. WHITTAKER

San Francisco bound passengers on all Santa Fe trains between 1933-1939 reached rails end at the Southern Pacific Oakland Mole, a great wooden trainshed. Transfer was made to a waddling ferry for the short trip across the bay to the big city. In the view above, a Santa Fe train rolls into SP's 16th Street Station with the Red Electric tracks on the left. (LEFT) The Pullman *Lone Lake* brings up the rear of the *Scout* as No. 3453 on the headend clears the big cut at Pinole.

FRED MATTHEWS

The California gold rush originally took Stockton by storm, then agricultural products from the fertile San Joaquin Valley. Streaking through Stockton under a cloud of smoke exhaust, the *Grand Canyon Limited* prepares to cross the Southern Pacific mainline. (BELOW) Trudging slowly down the center of the street in Fresno, an Atlantic and a Pacific type locomotive roll the eastbound *Scout* toward the station.

Doubleheaded redball manifest on the right rolls through Pinole at a fast clip. (BELOW) With 73-inch drivers digging into the steel rails, the long freight clatters across Franklin Canyon trestle then disappears into the mile long Franklin tunnel. (UPPER-LEFT) The way freight crosses the Southern Pacific Coalinga Branch at Hanford. (LOWER-LEFT) Something of the sound and fury of a freight getting under way is illustrated as No. 1462 thunders out of Calwa Yard in Fresno. The once proud Atlantic downgraded to a lowly freight "hog" still did a days work on the Riverbank local.

FRED MATTHEWS

The Oakdale Branch local often left Riverbank several times a week during the age of steam behind a time-honored 2-8-0. Traffic was exchanged with the classic Sierra Railroad at Oakdale, the last California common carrier to list steam on its roster. (BELOW) At the Oakdale station, Sierra Railroad No. 34 stands like a knight of olden time as it belches a few puffs of steam exhaust beside the Santa Fe's diesel mouse.

Engine terminal and yards at Richmond, end of the line for Santa Fe on the east-shore of San Francisco Bay. Freight bound for San Francisco is ferried across the bay on a large rail barge piloted by Santa Fe tugs. The town of Richmond was established in 1899, when the Santa Fe purchased a right-of-way to the bay-shore. Today Richmond has built up around the railroad and is a large industrial and residential community. (CENTER) A freight drag in from Stockton pulls into busy Richmond yard. (LOWER) The out of fashion motor inspection car based at Richmond. It must have presented a rare sight to see this machine coming down the track.

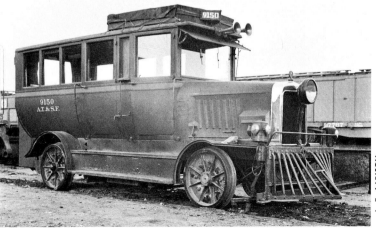

Bakersfield is spread along the south end of the San Joaquin Valley and from the foothills that string on both sides comes the oil that has made Bakersfield an important center. Between the rich oil fields are ranches of cotton, alfalfa, vineyards and citrus orchards. The Santa Fe established a large engine terminal here in the early days, housing the light engines for valley service and the big helpers for the Tehachapi grade. (ABOVE) A turn of the century passenger train pauses at Kern Junction in Bakersfield for orders. From here the Santa Fe uses jointly the Southern Pacific iron over Tehachapi to Mojave. The engineer inspects his air reservoir on the big Rhode Island built 4-6-0 before taking on the hill. (UPPER-LEFT) A doubleheader eases out of Bakersfield and soon will bite into the curving tracks that rise swiftly into the lofty Tehachapi Mountains. On the point is No. 651, one of 77 locomotives built by the Santa Fe in their own shops. (LOWER-LEFT) The venerable No. 374 began life as Atlantic & Pacific No. 74 in 1887. In this 1902 view, the classic 4-6-0 takes on water in the Bakersfield yard.

The engineer of the famous *California Limited* signs in at Redondo Junction roundhouse and reads the road assignment sheet. The engine for the days run from Los Angeles Union Passenger Terminal to Barstow was marked down as No. 3743. (BELOW) No. 3743 is spotted on the ready track beside the turntable. (UPPER-RIGHT) The fireman gives the brake hanger a bit of oil alongside the immense 69-inch drivers. (LOWER-RIGHT) The engineer glances down his trim machine waiting for the iron horse to drink its fill.

Going about its occasions, the San Bernardino local picks up speed after crossing the Los Angeles River. (RIGHT) All the wistful loneliness of a departing train is wonderfully captured at the Highgrove station. (LEFT) A winter scene near Los Angeles where snow-capped mountain peaks framed by the gold and green tints of the orange provide a rich background for the palm lined Santa Fe Route.

Tall stately palms that rustle gently with every breeze dot the landscape of Los Angeles and line the Santa Fe right-of-way with tropical
beauty. Santa Fe's Northern type locomotives were huge and tireless
creatures. They could and did cover the 1,765 miles between Kansas
City and Los Angeles without change, conquer Cajon and Raton, and
exceed 100 miles per hour.

By the light of the Pasadena station platform, a red cap takes a breather before the westbound *Chief* pulls in with a wagon load of baggage. Waiting its turn at the high iron, the local freight throbs on the siding. (RIGHT) A lone teen-ager wearing Bermuda shorts, crew socks and sneakers, is impressed by the glowing stainless steel cars and big red and silver diesel locomotive of the *Chief*.

G. M. BEST

Needles is a sub-tropical oasis on the desert and a large division point on the Santa Fe. The city seeks shelter from the sweltering heat in the shade of big palm and cottonwood trees. (ABOVE) A powerful 4-8-2 rolls the green cars of the eastbound *Chief* down the mainline toward Needles in the day when streamliners were unknown. (LEFT) The Needles roundhouse was busy in 1922. Note 16 engines in the house and one on the table. (LOWER) The same roundhouse as viewed in 1945. (BOTTOM) The *San Francisco Chief* pulls alongside the Needles station on the way East.

AL PHILLIPS C. KAUKE

170

With extension stack in erect position, the *Fast Mail & Express* smokes the hot summer sky as it digs out of Needles behind No. 2925, a roller-bearing 4-8-4 of wartime manufacture. The extension stack assisted in raising the smoke high enough to keep it from drifting into the cab. (CENTER) The train behind No. 3187 heads into Midland, near the banks of the Colorado River at Blythe on the "Parker Cutoff". (LOWER) Pure black smoke pours from the stack of No. 3900 as it assists a blue and yellow diesel drag across the desert at Java.

As long as steam lasted, the engineer in the visored cap riding behind the hurricane of power was envied beyond most. He was the overlord of the loud, dirty, hot, bouncing world of banging metal, steam and smoke of which the bystander seldom conceived.

THE STEAM LOCOMOTIVES

Locomotive No. 222 is typical of the early *Ten-Wheeler* type that pulled the fast passenger trains from the East to California in the 1890's and early 1900's. The later 4-6-0 type numbered in the 300 and 400 series, (some of which were compounds) ended their days on San Joaquin Valley passenger locals. The last of this type were scrapped in 1939.

Shown at Bakersfield in 1917, locomotive No. 686 is representative of the early *Consolidation* type built in large numbers between 1897 and 1902. These 2-8-0 engines were numbered in the 600, 700, 800 and 990 series. They were used in freight service and as yard engines throughout California. A number of them were rebuilt to 0-8-0 switchers in the early 1930's. All were scrapped by 1954, excepting No. 664 which is preserved at Los Angeles. Five others are displayed in the East.

The 2-10-2 type locomotive was first built for the Santa Fe, thereby earning the title *Santa Fe* type. Santa Fe enginemen preferred to call them "Big Mikes". One hundred fifty-nine of these were built for the AT&SF from 1903 to 1907 as tandem compounds (Nos. 900-984, 1600-1673). The 1912 view of No. 928 in Los Angeles shows the slightly canted tandem cylinders with the high-pressure cylinder forward and the low-pressure directly behind. Notice the extremely light connecting rods and the swing-out hoist attached to the smokebox. These powerful brutes handled the mainline freights over the deserts and mountains. Sometimes as many as six of them were strung out in a train climbing Cajon or Tehachapi. Between 1917 and 1924 they were all converted to single-expansion engines. The 1947 view of No. 972 near Corona shows how these locomotives looked toward the end of their days when they filled in on work trains, helpers and yard engines. All were scrapped by 1956 excepting No. 940, now on display at Bartlesville, Oklahoma.

Articulated compound No. 3299, a 2-8-8-0, was a Santa Fe experiment conceived in 1911. As with the 2-10-10-2's built that same year, the rear high-pressure unit was built from an existing engine, in this case a 1950 class 2-8-0. The front low-pressure unit was purchased new from Baldwin. Only four of these were built, and were used mainly as helpers on Cajon and Tehachapi. In 1923 all were rebuilt back into conventional 2-8-0's.

173

Engine No. 1262 typifies the early 4-6-2 *Pacific* type adopted by the Santa Fe. The 1226 class (Nos. 1226-1266) were built as balanced compounds in 1905-06. Many of them were rebuilt simple in the 1920's. Used mainly in the San Joaquin Valley, their 73-inch diameter drivers allowed them to handle passenger or fast freight assignments equally well. A few of these spent some time around Los Angeles and on the San Diego line during the 1930's. All were scrapped by 1950.

No. 1967 at Bakersfield in 1947. Most of the 1950 class (Nos. 1950-1991) worked in California at one time or another. Built by Baldwin in 1907, they were used in general freight service both on the Los Angeles and Valley divisions until bumped aside by the more powerful 2-8-2 and 2-10-2 types. Most of them ended their days on locals and in yard service. All were scrapped by 1955, with the exception of one preserved in Oklahoma.

The 1337 class (Nos. 1337-1388) *Pacifics* were the predominant passenger locomotives in California for a number of years. Built as balanced compounds in 1912-13, all were converted to simple engines in the 1920's. They worked the Los Angeles-Needles, San Diego, and Valley mainlines, and as helpers at Needles until replaced by the more powerful 4-8-2 and 4-8-4 types. Many ended their days as Valley freight engines. All were scrapped by 1954. The later 3400 class 4-6-2's were uncommon in California, although six were used in the Valley during the 1940's.

No. 2103 is typical of the venerable 0-6-0 "yard goat" that could be found in every yard of any size in California. These spunky switchers were hard at work around the clock in San Francisco, Los Angeles and San Diego. In the 1930's diesels made their first inroads into the ranks of the switchers. The 2000 and 2100 series engines that were left by 1946 were renumbered 9000's and 9100's. All were scrapped by 1955, excepting No. 9005 preserved at Clovis, New Mexico.

Locomotive No. 1468 was a common sight between Los Angeles and San Bernardino for many years. It regularly handled the three-car "San Berdoo" local, a daily mail train between these two cities. Between stops, the big 79-inch drivers would really accelerate the short train. Other *Atlantics* subbed for diesels on the Valley *Golden Gates* and a couple worked local freights there until the end of steam. All these 4-4-2's were scrapped by 1953.

No. 3527 at San Bernardino in 1919 shows the balanced compound 4-6-2's as they looked before conversion to single expansion locomotives. Arriving in 1914, the 3500 class (Nos. 3500-3534) were the last compounds built for the Santa Fe. Mostly used in California passenger service during the 1920-30 era. Like the 1200 and 1300 series, they too were pushed aside by newer and heavier engines. All were scrapped by 1955.

3450 class (Nos. 3450-3459). Five of these racy *Hudsons* were assigned to Valley passenger runs during the 1940's, and occasionally wandered down to the Los Angeles division. They handled trains at better than 100 mph in the Valley, but it was not uncommon to see one climbing Tehachapi with a short train. Nos. 3450, 3458 and 3459 each obtained large tenders in 1951-52. All were scrapped by 1956, excepting the 3450. It is preserved by the R&LHS at Pomona. The later 3460 class 4-6-4's were not regularly used in California.

No. 3156 is a good example of the 3129 class *Mikado* type, (Nos. 3129-3158) out-shopped in 1916. Almost all of these medium-sized 2-8-2's called the Los Angeles division their home during their career. They could handle just about anything—drag, local, work train, helper. They were quite common on the San Diego line and on locals between San Bernardino and Los Angeles. Replaced by the heavier 3160 and 4000 class Mikes toward the end of steam here, those remaining on the roster were sent East. All 3129 class were scrapped by 1954.

3765 class (Nos. 3765-3775). These eleven 4-8-4 *Northern* type were designed by Santa Fe mechanical officers and built in 1937 at the Baldwin Works. They included the latest appliances and were massive from any angle. The locomotive alone weighed just under 250 tons. With the excellent performances the new 3765's turned in, previous 4-8-4's (Nos. 3751-3764) were soon rebuilt to match them. The 3765 class handled most of the overland passenger trains to California, sharing the load with the 3751's and later the 3776 class (Nos. 3776-3785). Nos. 3751, 3759 and 3768 are the only locomotives of these classes to have been preserved.

Engine No. 3747 shown at Pasadena in 1949. The 3700 class (Nos. 3700-3750) 4-8-2 *Mountain* type were the mainstays for the overland passenger trains from the twenties until the modern 4-8-4 type was developed in the late 1930's. All of the 3700's that were oil-burners were used in California, replacing the 1300 series *Pacifics* as passenger trains grew longer and heavier. Their 69-inch drivers made them suitable also for fast freight service, and many spent their last days in Valley freight pools. All were scrapped by 1955.

2900 class (Nos. 2900-2929). The last steam passenger power built for the Santa Fe in 1944. These exceptional locomotives called the Needles-Los Angeles-San Diego mainlines their "beat" for the waning years of steam in California. They had roller bearings on all rods and axles and were capable of speeds over 100 mph. They turned in some exceptional mileage records—many running through from Los Angeles to Kansas City with only intermediate servicing. Last used in Texas and Oklahoma freight service, all were scrapped by 1960 except No. 2921 which is on display at Modesto and five others preserved in the East.

No. 3881 at Victorville in 1947. The 3800 class (Nos. 3800-3940) were the latest Santa Fe 2-10-2 design. Built by Baldwin between 1919 and 1927, they were the prime freight hauling locomotive in Southern California, giving up their domain only when the big blue and yellow diesels finally outnumbered them. Their exhausts echoed off Cajon Pass for the last time in the summer of 1952. Not one of the 3800's were saved, all meeting the torch by 1956.

Foundation of the yard, like everything else about a railroad is track — tracks arranged in clusters or groups for reception of freight trains or individual cars loaded by shippers. The 1st Street Yard in Los Angeles shown above is a beehive of activity on a warm summers morning. The *San Diegan* has just left Los Angeles Union Passenger Terminal and is caught racing along the cement bank of the Los Angeles River. On the left, a freight bound for the 1st Street Yard passes the *Grand Canyon Limited* on the fly. (LOWER) A switchman gives the signal to push a cut of mechanical refrigerator cars through the yard tracks.

Once a desert junction for overland wagon trains, Barstow is now the junction for the largest diesel repair facility on the Santa Fe system. Although built back in 1945, at the beginning of large scale dieselization, Barstow shops were planned for expansion. Night and day the diesels move in and out of the shops shown above. On the left, an electrician checks the headlight wiring, while below, the famous *El Capitan* pulls into Barstow yard under a mantle of electric floodlights.

SANTA FE RAILWAY—FRANK E. MEITZ

SANTA FE RAILWAY—R. COLLINS BRADLEY

Since the inauguration of the *Super Chief* in 1936, the Santa Fe has been building its mainline tracks into a modern steel highway. The laying of hundreds of miles of new heavier rail, inserting longer ties and reballasting goes on all year long. The Santa Fe has been able to keep its railroad in good shape despite economic stresses and strains and the up-grading goes on. In the view above, the surveyor checks the grade on Cajon Pass where the westbound mainline crosses over the eastbound. Navajo Indians have always proved highly satisfactory as section crews. On the left, a group of Indians tamp ballast on Cajon. On the page to the right, welded rail is being put through a threader which places it between the rails near Cajon station. The crane is used to float single sections of rail into place. A Navajo track gang pound home the spikes on the far right.

The freight conductor in the cupola of a modern Santa Fe mainline freight can communicate with the engineer of his own train or crew in the diesel or caboose of the passing train by radio-telephone. On the right, a long train of "Piggyback" truck-trailers roll over Tehachapi Pass enroute to the East. (TOP-RIGHT) Automatic color light signals on the Centralized Traffic Control board, like unsleeping sentinels, stand watch by day and by night over the many miles of Santa Fe tracks in California. (LOWER-RIGHT) To speed the handling of mail, the Santa Fe inaugurated a containerized trailer-type operation which eliminates delays in terminal handling.

SANTA FE RAILWAY—R. COLLINS BRADLEY

BOTH SANTA FE RAILWAY

181

The Santa Fe's navy on San Francisco Bay
has grown since 1929 from four tugs with
3,000 horsepower to five tugs aggregating
4,800 horsepower. One steel tug, the
Edward J. Engel, named for a Santa Fe
president, can be seen above as she heads
across the bay into the setting sun with a
barge securely tied to her starboard side.
Another still larger tug was placed in service during 1947, bearing the name *John R.
Hayden.* On the left, crew of the Hayden
go about their duties of handling the helm
and tying the tug to the barge. On the right,
a deck hand prepares to release the car
barrier.

The last great movement of the symphony of steam thunders to climactic splendor on Cajon Pass. Only memories on celluloid remind one of the Golden Age of Railroading.

DONALD DUKE

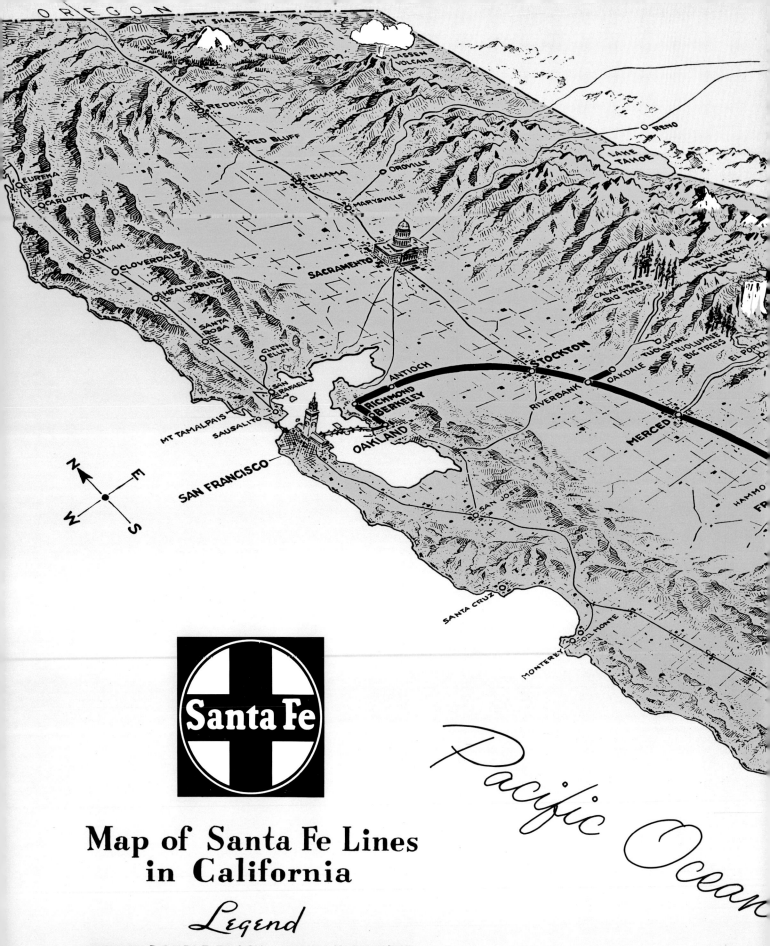

Map of Santa Fe Lines in California

Legend

=O=O= DOUBLE TRACK ——— HIGHWAYS

●●●● Motor Route Co-ordinated with Train Service